D1243461

MODERN WORLD NATIONS

MODERN WORLD NATIONS

Colombia
Updated Edition

Charles F. Gritzner
South Dakota State University

CHELSEA HOUSE
An Infobase Learning Company

Frontispiece: Flag of Colombia

Cover: Downtown Bogota, Colombia

Colombia

Chelsea House
An imprint of Infobase Learning
132 West 31st Street
New York NY 10001

The Library of Congress has catalogued the earlier edition as follows:
Gritzner, Charles F.
  Colombia / Charles F. Gritzner.
    p. cm.—(Modern world nations)
  Includes bibliographical references and index.
  ISBN-13: 978–0-7910–9509–6 (hardcover)
  ISBN-10: 0–7910–9509–6 (hardcover)
  1. Colombia—Juvenile literature I. Title. II. Series.

  F2258.5.G75 2007
  986.1—dc22

2007026409

ISBN 978-1-61753-045-6

Series design by Takeshi Takahashi
Cover design by Takeshi Takahashi
Cover printed by Yurchak Printing, Landisville, Pa.
Book printed and bound by Yurchak Printing, Landisville, Pa.
Printed in the United States of America

Table of Contents

Colombia

CHAPTER

1

Introducing Colombia

"Coast Guard Hauls in 20 Tons of Cocaine in Record Bust"; "Colombia Finds 211 Bodies in Mass Graves"; "Colombia Leads World in [Land] Mine Victims"; "Colombia Orders More Lawmakers Arrested"; "12 Hostages Plea for Help in Colombia." For most Latin American countries, even those with a history of instability, it would take decades, if not centuries, to generate news headlines as alarming as these, but not Colombia. The events described here (taken from various news services) all occurred within several weeks in the spring of 2007. They speak volumes of the human tragedy that grips this tropical South American country. During the latter half of the twentieth century, many Latin American countries experienced civil turmoil. During the past decade, however, only Colombia was troubled by chaos and violence on such a massive scale.

By 2010, there were many signs of improvement. Political turmoil was subsiding. A mid-year election resulted in a peaceful presidential transition in which Juan Manuel Santos replaced popular Alvaro Uribe who had served two four-year terms of office. The firm grip of terrorist organizations on the country and its people was weakened. The Uribe administration took a very strong stand against the illegal drug trade, resulting in a weakening of cartels and a decline in the production and trade of drugs. Guerrilla forces and other terrorist groups had brought decades of chaos and bloodshed to the country, yet their influence, too, has declined during recent years.

Colombia, by any measure, should be a prosperous country. Its location at the northwestern tip of South America makes it the closest of that continent's lands to the United States. This geographic position favors the further development of trade and commerce between the two countries. Colombia has excellent port facilities on both the Atlantic and Pacific oceans—the only South American country that has this advantage. The airline distance from Miami, Florida, to Colombia's tropical coast is about the same as from Miami to Dallas–Fort Worth, Texas. Were the country to stabilize, it would be a wonderful tourist destination for *norteamericanos* (the preferred term for residents of the United States and Canada).

Colombia has a diversified economy based on sustainable agriculture, as well as logging, mining, manufacturing, and a growing service sector. With nearly 45 million people, it has the third largest population in all of Latin America, trailing only Brazil and Mexico. About 92 percent of the population is literate, which is extremely important in a postindustrial global age. Located in the northern Andes, Colombia's tropical location is modified by highlands and their cooling effect. In fact, most of the country's people live in upland basins that are lands of "eternal spring."

Given the conditions described in the preceding paragraph, one can but wonder, "What went wrong?" Many answers can be found in the headlines that opened this chapter. For nearly a half century, Colombia has been a leading

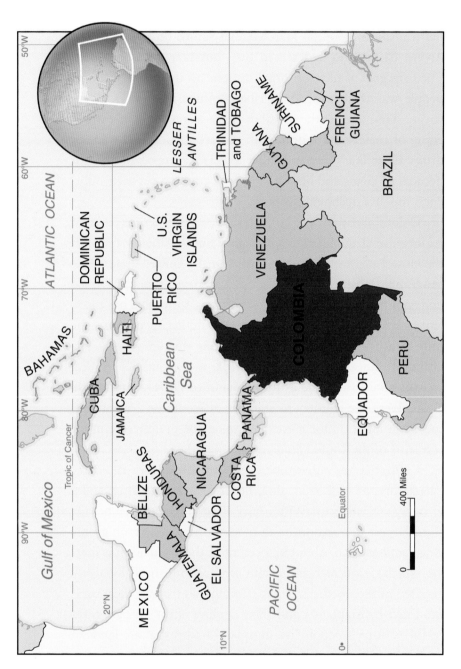

The Republic of Colombia is located in the northwestern part of South America and shares borders with the countries of Panama, to the northwest; Venezuela, to the east; Brazil, to the southeast; Peru, to the south; and Ecuador, to the southwest. In addition, the Caribbean Sea borders Colombia to the north and the Pacific Ocean borders it to the west.

producer and distributor of cocaine. Today, although illegal and undocumented, drugs are certainly the country's chief source of foreign revenue. One can gain some idea of the value of this illegal industry from the estimated $600 million street value of the record drug bust cited. Because of the vast wealth to be made from this illegal trade, many criminal groups have become involved in its production and marketing. For nearly 50 years, various guerrilla forces, paramilitary groups, and organized crime lords have waged a heated war against one another, seeking an upper hand in controlling the lucrative drug trade.

When conducting illegal activities, it is helpful to hold influence over the government—politicians, the military, and police. Drug cartels (organizations), with their vast financial resources, find that many politicians can easily be bribed. The result is rampant corruption and a government that, until recently at least, many believed to be controlled by and protective of the drug lords. In this unstable environment, crime continues to be widespread. From 2000 to 2004, the last period for which data was available, Colombia was the world leader among ranked countries in murders and kidnappings. Although conditions appear to have improved during recent years, it is little wonder that most citizens continue to live in constant fear for their lives.

In an attempt to stem the tide of the drug trade, the United States has become deeply involved in supporting the (currently) friendly Colombian government. In fact, the country receives more foreign aid each year from the United States than any other country outside the Middle East.

Finally, as if all of these human-induced hardships were not enough, Colombia is also subject to various natural hazards. Periodic earthquakes and volcanic eruptions take a severe toll on property and human life. In addition, the Caribbean coastal plain is subject to seasonal droughts.

Has Colombia's situation always been like this? No. Will Colombia continue to be ravaged by heated conflicts in the

With a population of nearly 9 million, Bogotá is Colombia's largest city and also its capital. Located in the Andes Mountains, at 8,661 feet (2,640 meters) above sea level, the city is one of the highest capitals in the world.

years to come? It is difficult to say. The data (see the "Facts at a Glance" section at the end of the book) suggest that Colombia is in a much better position to prosper than are many other Latin American countries. The natural environment, although presenting some challenges, offers considerable potential for future economic development and human settlement. Today, because of the conflict and chaos that are rampant throughout most of the country, many rural areas have been drained of population. People flee to the cities in search of a safe haven. Few people are left behind to develop the environmental economic potentials of the rural areas.

With the arrival of the Spaniards in the early sixteenth century, Colombia experienced the clash of European and Amerindian cultures that occurred throughout the Americas. However there is nothing about this collision, or the colonial experience that followed, that sets Colombia apart from most other countries within the region. In terms of population and culture, Colombia does not stand out in any unique way. The balance of Spaniards, *mestizos* (those of mixed Spanish and Amerindian descent), Indians, Afro-Colombians, and others is comparable to that of many other Latin American countries. The diversity of peoples has not been a primary factor in creating social conflict.

The country is struggling, both politically and with its "legal" economy. Problems in both sectors can be attributed primarily to the drug trade and power of the various militant groups that have terrorized the country for decades. Despite the many problems that its people face, however, in 2009, Colombia ranked seventy-seventh among 182 countries rated in the Human Development Index (HDI). (The Human Development Index is a comparative measure of life expectancy, literacy, education, and standard of living for countries worldwide. It is used by the United Nations.) In this measure of human well-being, 17 Latin American countries (many of which are small Caribbean islands) rank higher than Colombia. Nonetheless, the country's ranking places it roughly in the middle among the region's states and in the upper fourth among less-developed countries (LDCs).

In this book, you will visit the lands, peoples, and regions of this country with a name that honors Christopher Columbus. During your travels, you will learn more about the problems Colombia faces and also about the country's great potential for growth and development. Your tour will begin with an overview of Colombia's natural environment and its varied physical landscapes.

2

Physical Landscapes

Colombia is both blessed and hindered by its physical geographic conditions. Its location places it squarely in the tropical latitudes, an environment that can be challenging in many ways. Most potential effects of a tropical environment, though, are lessened by Columbia's large expanse of cooler, more pleasant, and healthful highlands. Towering mountains divide the country's population into separate and somewhat isolated groups. Consequently, within the valleys between the ranges, inhabitants have developed their own distinctive regional character. Coastal lowlands and a broad interior plain make up two-thirds of the country; mountains make up the remainder. These are just some of the physical conditions that make Colombia unique among Latin American countries. This chapter describes and explains the country's major physical features and their importance.

LANDFORMS

Changes in elevation offer a wide variety of places for Colombian people to live, plants and wildlife to thrive, and agricultural crops to grow. The topography and resulting diversity of physical landscapes has influenced Colombia's history, economy, and settlement. The cooler mountain air provides a sharp contrast to the hot, humid, insect-infested tropical lowlands. Changes in elevation highlight the landform regions of Colombia: the coast, Andes Mountains, and *Oriente* (Spanish for "East"). Each region's physical geography and natural resources have contributed to the development of Colombia.

Coastal Zones

Colombia is the only country in South America that faces both the Pacific and Atlantic (Caribbean) coasts. Together, the narrow Pacific and Atlantic coastal zones make up less than 10 percent of Colombia's total land area. The Pacific Coast subregion includes a narrow coastal plain, a first-class natural harbor, a range of relatively low mountains, and a low depression. The sole natural harbor is the pouch-shaped setting for Buenaventura, the country's only large Pacific coastal town and seaport. The Baudó Range (Serranía del Baudó) is the Pacific Coast's solitary range of mountains. They rise out of the sea. Their sharp-crested peaks actually begin in Panama and pass along the entire west coast of Colombia. Geologically, the Baudó Range is not part of or as high as the Andes Mountains, but it includes some of the most rugged terrain in all of Colombia.

A pass through the range connects Buenaventura by highway and railroad to a low depression. Geographers call this lowland, a narrow arch of low marshes and swamps, the Chocó. It is not entirely in the Pacific Ocean's realm; the Chocó stretches from the Pacific to the Caribbean. The San Juan and Atrato rivers drain the lowland. The San Juan flows into the Pacific and the Atrato into the Caribbean. In the late nineteenth

Colombia's topography is quite diverse: It includes swampy lowlands in the west, majestic mountain ranges such as the 18,000-foot-plus (5,486-meter-plus) volcanic Cordillera Central in the interior, and the savanna grasslands of the Llano region in the east. The country also is part of the Pacific "Ring of Fire," with several active volcanoes, primarily in the Cordillera Central region.

century, European engineers considered this soggy depression as a possible route for an interocean ship canal. They eventually abandoned the idea, though, because they decided that building a canal there would cost too much money. In the early twentieth century, U.S. engineers would finally build such a canal, but they chose to dig it across Panama (Colombia's Central American neighbor to the northwest).

At the beginning of the sixteenth century, the Spanish made Colombia's Caribbean coast their main gateway for settlement on *tierra firme*, present-day northwestern South America, Central America, and the western Caribbean. A close examination of a map of the coastline reveals four large natural harbors. Three became sites of early coastal ports and entry points for inland settlement and trade. The most westerly harbor is the Gulf of Urabá. This raindrop-shaped bay will never become a first-class harbor because it is too shallow for large ships. As a result, to this day, it does not have a major port town. In contrast, the next two harbors to the east are large seaports. Cartagena, which is the site of an important colonial fortress, is the next harbor to the east, while Barranquilla, which is just northeast of Cartagena, is the country's most important seaport. The fourth and most easterly harbor is the site of Santa Marta, the oldest city in Colombia.

The Santa Marta Mountains (*Sierra Nevada de Santa Marta*) rise out of the Caribbean and overlook the city of Santa Marta. This range is impressive for its cloud-shrouded summits, some of which reach nearly 19,000 feet (5,800 meters) above sea level. The mountainous area has a colorful history of coffee cultivation and illegal marijuana production. The Guajira Peninsula, which juts into the Caribbean Sea, makes up the extreme northeast coast. Colombia shares an international border along the full length of the peninsula with Venezuela. As we shall see, this dreary piece of land has become a haven for drug traffickers because of its remoteness and strategic location on a key drug-trafficking route to North America and Europe.

Stretching approximately 950 miles (1,540 kilometers) north to south, the Magdalena is Colombia's longest river. Named after the Christian saint Mary Magdalene, the river is a vital trade route that connects the coastal regions of the north with the mountains of the interior.

The Caribbean plain, which extends inland from the coast, makes up the remainder of the Caribbean coast subregion. Most of this area is drained by the Magdalena River. This waterway begins as a steep torrent in the Andes, slows down as it crosses the nearly flat coastal plain, and empties sluggishly into the Caribbean Sea near Barranquilla. Along its route from the Andes, it collects water from the smaller streams that join it. By the time it reaches the coastal plain, the Magdalena River is huge and, as a result, is prone to flooding. Floods occur each year during the rainy season, so much so that the river hampers settlement of the plain. Nevertheless, the Magdalena and its main tributary, the Cauca River, are vital routes for trade between the coastal seaports and the resource-rich Andes Mountains.

The Andes Mountains

Colombia includes the northern end of the magnificent Andes Mountains. Geographers usually refer to the range simply as the Andes. The Andes mark the western margin of both Colombia and the rest of the South American continent. They are a grand system of mountain ranges, interrupted by north- to south-trending valleys. The mountains' geologic complexity is evident in their wavy layers of gray and pink lava, red and brown sandstone, creamy marble, and speckled granite. The rugged beauty of the Andes is a product of both past and ongoing volcanic activity, geologic uplift, and erosion. Andean uplift occurs because tectonic plates (large sections of Earth's outer rock layer) in the region are colliding. The collision usually involves a large, westward-moving South American Plate and the smaller eastward-moving Nazca Plate. The advancing edge of the South American Plate lifts upward as it crashes against the smaller oceanic plates. This collision causes rocks to fold and break along faults. Volcanism and earthquakes (movements along the faults) accompany the uplift.

Three ranges make up the Colombian Andes: Western (Occidental), Central (Central), and Eastern (Oriental). These ranges open and fan out northward from the Pasto Knot, a mountainous zone in the southwestern part of the country. Between the Western and Central ranges flows the Cauca River. The Magdalena River, which the Cauca joins, separates the Central and Eastern ranges on its long journey to the Caribbean Sea. The Central Range (*Cordillera Central*) is the highest of Colombia's three major ranges. Several spectacular volcanic peaks rise more than 18,000 feet (about 5,500 meters). This range is notorious for its dangerous volcanoes. In 1985, the cone-shaped Nevado del Ruiz volcano erupted violently, killing more than 23,000 people. It remains the deadliest volcanic eruption ever to occur in South America.

The Eastern Range (*Cordillera Oriental*) lies east of the Magdalena River. It is the broadest of the three mountain groups. There, high, snowcapped peaks frame picturesque, flat-bottomed basins. The basins are large and have served as the magnet for human settlement because of their size, favorable elevations, freshwater lakes, fertile volcanic soils, and grassy plains. The Bogotá basin, home of the national capital, is the largest and most populous valley. The Western Range (*Cordillera Occidental*) lies west of the Cauca River. This highland region is the least spectacular of the three ranges. It is lower in elevation and has neither prominent volcanoes or basins, nor major cities.

Glaciers can be found on a few peaks in the Cordillera Central, Cordillera Oriental, and Sierra Nevada de Santa Marta. Snowfields and glaciers require continually cold temperatures during a period of centuries to develop. In the warm, tropical latitudes of equatorial Colombia, these conditions can only occur on the highest peaks. Colombia's glaciers are few in number, but their creation, descriptions by early Spanish explorers, and present distribution tell scientists something about climatic change. Glaciers are masses of moving ice that begin as snowfields, which are permanent layers of snow. The snowfields grow only if there is an accumulation of snowfall during a long period of time. Eventually, if snow accumulation proceeds from one year to the next, solid ice begins to form in the snowfields' deepest layers. This ice layer becomes so thick—anywhere from 50 to 200 feet (30 to 60 meters)—that gravity causes it to move outward from its deepest part. (The movement is similar to how pancake batter poured on a hot skillet spreads outward from its center.)

As a glacier moves down a mountain, it grinds, gouges, and grooves the surrounding walls and floor to create a deep, U-shaped valley and other types of glacial landforms. The Spanish named snowcapped peaks is *nevada(o)* (which means "snow-covered" or "snowy" in Spanish). An example of such a peak is Nevado del Ruiz. Today, Nevado del Ruiz has a glacier, but many peaks that the Spanish named nevada(o) no longer have snowfields. Scientists have identified landforms and telltale markings left behind by glaciers on the "nevada(o)" peaks, confirming that they were aptly named by the early Spanish settlers.

Based on the evidence of former snowfields and glaciers, scientists have concluded that glaciers were more widespread when the Spanish arrived 500 years ago than they are today. They believe that a warmer climate since the Spanish settlers' arrival stopped the accumulation of leftover winter snow and ice that formed the glaciers. As a result, they say, the glaciers melted rapidly and disappeared. The findings are part of the growing body of knowledge from many parts of the world that supports the theory that Earth's global climate is warming. It also casts some doubt on the so-called "greenhouse effect" that attributes global warming to human causes. Nature, after all, constantly undergoes climatic change, and a growing number of scientists now believe that Earth simply is in a normal warming cycle.

The Oriente

The Oriente, or Eastern Tropical Lowland, is a low plain that makes up roughly two-thirds of the eastern part of the country. Rivers have separated its flat surface into sections, so that Colombians often refer to the region in plural form as the *Llanos* (Spanish for "the plains"). The plain tilts gently downward from the base of the Andes. Meandering rivers flowing from the mountains have deposited thick layers of sediment to form this flatland. A low, hilly area sneaks eastward across this plateau from the Andes, dividing the stream drainage into two parts. The rivers to the north of the divide flow into the Orinoco River, which drains Venezuela and flows into the Atlantic Ocean. Rivers south of the divide flow into the mighty Amazon River, which passes through Brazil before emptying into the Atlantic.

Savanna grassland covers most of the northern half of the Oriente, making this part of the country important for grazing cattle. Tropical rainforest covers the southern half of the region, but large-scale cattle ranching in the western extreme of this subregion has resulted in the clearing of vast expanses of forest.

The whole region has the nickname "cowboy country" because of the importance that cattle raising has to its economy. Sedimentary rocks lie beneath most of the plains. Some of these porous rocks store valuable deposits of oil and natural gas. These two energy resources make the Oriente important to Colombia's economy and economic future.

WEATHER AND CLIMATE

Colombia lies entirely in the tropics—in fact, the Equator passes through the southern part of the country—yet its climate varies from hot desert to frigid alpine conditions. The striking variety of climates can be attributed to differences in elevation and the effect elevation has on temperature and precipitation. It is often said that, "climate in Colombia is 'vertical.'" When traveling from low valleys to high mountains, air temperature decreases as elevation increases. As a result, the highest yearly average temperatures occur in the lowlands. For instance, the annual average temperature at Santa Marta, a coastal city, is 84°F (29°C), and at Barranquilla, another coastal city, it is 83°F (25°C). In the mountains, temperatures are noticeably cooler. For example, the annual average temperature of Bogotá, which lies about 8,661 feet (2,640 meters) above sea level, is 56°F (13°C). Snow occupies higher peaks year-round.

Alexander von Humboldt, a German geographer, was the first scientist to study the relationship between air temperature and elevation. He first studied this link in the northern Andes of Colombia. Humboldt arrived in Colombia at Cartagena in March 1801. At the time, the city was a great Spanish seaport. Before Humboldt departed from Europe, King Charles IV of Spain gave him and his colleague Aimé Bonpland (a French botanist) permission to visit the Spanish colonies in the New World. In return, the king asked Humboldt to report on the condition of the gold and silver mines in the colonies.

From Cartagena, the two scientists followed the Magdalena River upstream. They climbed the Andes Mountains to Bogotá. Humboldt and Bonpland finished their historic journey by going on to Quito (Ecuador) and then to Lima (Peru), Spain's principal seaport on the Pacific Ocean. Humboldt visited the Spanish mines in the area to satisfy the king's request, and during his ascent of the mountains, he identified three broad temperature zones made up of hot, temperate, and cold lands. Geographers still use Humboldt's concept of vertical zones of temperature to describe climates of all mountainous tropical regions, although the three zones vary slightly from place to place, depending upon local conditions.

In Colombia, the *tierra caliente* (Spanish for "hot land") begins in the lowlands and extends to an elevation of about 3,000 feet (915 meters). Temperatures in the tierra caliente range from 75°F (24°C) to 83°F (28°C). The *tierra templada* ("temperate land") is roughly 3,000 to 6,000 feet (915 to 1,829 meters), with readings from 65° to 77°F (18° to 25°C). The *tierra fria* ("cold land"), which lies above 6,000 feet (1,829 meters), has much lower temperatures than the temperate zone. Alpine conditions begin at roughly 10,000 feet (3,048 meters) with snow and glaciers on the highest peaks. Humboldt aptly noted that, regardless of elevation, air temperature in the tropics tends to vary little from month to month. For example, Santa Marta's thermal range is just 14°F (8°C) and Bogotá's is 23°F (13°C). In comparison, the seasonal temperature range of New York City, a location outside the tropics, is 45°F (25°C).

Precipitation is also important in classifying different climates. In the tropics, rainfall usually varies according to two seasons—high(er) sun and low(er) sun. (Because the sun is always quite high in the tropical sky and temperatures differ little from season to season, it really is an exaggeration to speak of "summer" and "winter.") Maximum rainfall occurs during the high sun period that extends from April through October. The lower sun period, November through March, is considerably drier.

Colombia does not experience real temperature seasons because of its equatorial location. The seasonal variations that do exist result from wind and precipitation patterns. Summer moisture for most of Colombia is delivered by the northeast trade winds. The winds contribute to a wet-and-dry tropical climate in the northern two-thirds of the country. Rainfall begins in April and May as the winds pick up water vapor from the warm Caribbean Sea and blow it toward South America's north coast. Arriving at the coast, the winds are full of moisture. There is not so much as a drizzle, however, until the winds pass inland, where they heat up and begin to rise. As the air rises, its temperature decreases to the point of condensation, causing giant thunderclouds and heavy showers. Torrential downpours are typical summer afternoon occurrences throughout the country. The northeast trade winds diminish in early November. As the winds move gradually eastward away from Colombia, the dry season sets in and lasts until March.

Rainfall totals in most of Colombia reflect this wet summer–dry winter pattern. For example, Barranquilla, a northern seaport, receives 34 inches (864 millimeters), but only 4 of those inches (102 millimeters) fall during the winter. The wet-and-dry effect of the northeast trades extends into the northern half of the Oriente ("Eastern") plains region. The Andes region also experiences the wet-and-dry seasonal rhythm. Bogotá, for instance, receives 33 inches (838 millimeters) of rainfall all year, but only 11 inches (278 millimeters) occurs in the winter.

Marked departures from the wet-and-dry rainfall pattern occur in two areas. The first area is the thin desert zone near part of the northern coastal fringe. Arid conditions begin along the coast near Santa Marta, which receives barely 13 inches (330 millimeters) of rainfall each year. They then stretch eastward to include the Guajira Peninsula, which receives less than 10 inches (250 millimeters). The moist northeast trades pass over this coast, but they usually lift to form clouds farther inland. Rare summer thundershowers account for the sparse precipitation. These small storms spring up every few days, but bring only momentary relief to the hot temperatures and extreme dryness of the region.

A second exception to the wet-and-dry seasonal rainfall pattern occurs in super humid portions of southern Colombia, which make up about a third of the country. These areas receive a lot of rainfall because they have a reliable source of moisture throughout the year. They include the Pacific Coastal Lowland, the Pasto Knot mountain region, and the southern Oriente plains. The wettest area in all of North and South America is Colombia's Chocó region, which averages more than 250 inches (6,500 millimeters) of rainfall each year. In fact, although still unofficial, it is possible that this soggy area holds the world record for the "wettest place." The sleepy village of Lloro reportedly averages 524 inches (13,310 millimeters) of rainfall per year, a whopping 57 inches (1,448 millimeters) more than the current official record holder! Elsewhere, Popayán, a city in the Pasto Knot region, receives an average 77 inches (1,956 millimeters) of rain each year. Leticia, a city in the southern Oriente area and Colombia's only port on the Amazon River, averages 111 inches (2,819 millimeters) of rainfall annually.

In addition to the trade winds, mountain ranges also affect rainfall patterns. They block moisture-carrying winds to create "rain shadows," or areas of less rainfall, in wind-sheltered valleys and basins. For example, the climate of a small upper section of the Magdalena River valley is actually a desert because little rain reaches it. As a result, the valley floor has thorny bushes, cacti, and agave vegetation, whereas the surrounding mountains support lush mountain rainforests. Another example of a rain shadow is the Bogotá basin. The adjoining ranges receive at least twice the amount of precipitation that Bogotá does.

PLANTS AND SOILS

If you were to fly over Colombia in a jetliner on a cloudless day, most of the country would look like someone had covered it with a dark green velvet cloth. The Andes would be rumpled folds, appearing smooth as you flew over the Caribbean lowlands and Oriente. Much of the country would have a green hue because of Colombia's natural vegetation, which is mainly tropical rainforest.

Natural vegetation, or flora, depends primarily on two important elements of the physical environment: climate and soil. Sunlight, temperature, and precipitation establish the natural limits of growth for various plants. As a result, each climate type tends to have just one or two dominant plant communities. Climate is also very important to soil development. It affects the rate of rock weathering (decomposition or disintegration into fine particles), overlying vegetation, erosion, and leaching (the removal of soil nutrients by water).

Soil is vital to plants because it can limit the nutrients and water that plants need in order to grow. Nutrients come from the tiny particles of clay, silt, and sand that comprise the soil, as well as from organic matter, or decaying plant and animal tissue. Soil also stores water that plants need to survive. A soil's depth and texture (or particle size) affect the amount of moisture and food in the soil. For example, tropical rainforests have deep soils, abundant moisture, and plentiful organic matter on the surface. In contrast, desert soils are thin and hold only small amounts of organic matter and soil moisture.

Tropical rainforests thrive in the low, hot, wet tierra caliente zone. The forest's thick canopy of leaves and vines protects the deep soil from tropical heat and heavy rains. Unfortunately, Colombians have cleared away large areas of the lush forest and exposed the soil to water erosion and baking rays of the sun. As a result, Colombians are no longer able to grow crops, harvest timber, or even collect firewood in such areas. Geographers call the still forested area of this region the "Zone of Tropical Products" because carefully managed crops of cassavas (an edible root plant, also called *manioc*), sugarcane, bananas, and other water-demanding and warmth-loving plants can grow well there. Even so, forest clearing and soil erosion are serious problems. Some sizeable areas of the tropical rainforest still exist in

One of Colombia's primary environmental concerns is deforestation. According to a 2003 United Nations study, Colombia loses approximately 775 square miles (2,000 square kilometers) of land each year to such activities as small-scale agriculture and logging. Pictured here is a Colombian rainforest that has been cleared for farming.

parts of the Andes, Chocó, and southern Oriente, but they are shrinking. Certain slopes and valleys facing the northeast trade winds still have patches of this forest, even in the heavily populated areas of the Andes.

Savannas (tropical grasslands) grow in subhumid parts of the tierra caliente, such as the northern Oriente and Caribbean lowlands. These grasslands are one of nature's responses to tropical climates that have a wet-and-dry annual rainfall pattern. During the wet season, the grasses grow tall (waist high in many areas) and form a thick, protective layer over the soil. During the dry season, the grasses dry out. For thousands of years, the dead grasses have been burned simply to remove their useless mass. The result of burning is that most trees are killed, leaving an open environment in which grasses thrive.

Savannas are natural pasturelands, but overgrazing can lead to soil erosion. These grasslands are by no means tree free. Trees often grow along the banks and floodplains of the stream courses, where they are protected from fires. Drought-tolerant species of palms and other trees also grow scattered about the open plain. As noted, the sweeping grasslands of the Oriente make up Colombia's main cattle-ranching area, although extensive areas are overgrazed.

Desert plants grow in the *tierra caliente* where rainfall is too low to support savanna grasses. The Guajira Peninsula is such a location. Plants there are able to survive because they need only small amounts of nutrients and water. Desert grasses grow in widely spaced clumps. Certain small bushes are xerophytes (from Latin for "dry plants"). They have the ability to reduce moisture loss through leaves and stems. Other plants, such as cacti and agaves, are succulents. They have special "spongy" cells that store precious water. As in all dry lands, the amount of rainfall is meager, so farming is difficult, even in the most favorable localities. Some of the country's poorest farmers eke out a living in the arid Guajira region.

The *tierra templada* is pleasant for plants because the moderate elevations of 3,000 to 6,000 feet (915 to 1,829 meters) compensate for the high temperatures of the low latitudes. A lush evergreen cloud forest grows in this zone. Here, the dense forest creates a closed canopy. Below, colorful orchids, delicate ferns, and thousands of other plants grow. Vines hang from many trees, as do the dangling roots of epiphytes (plants that gain their nourishment from the air). Alluvial (stream) deposits create fertile soils in the valleys. The agreeable climate and fertile valleys of the Andes support Colombia's densest populations. Geographers refer to this region of South America as the "Coffee Zone" because coffee is a typical commercial crop grown there.

The *tierra fria,* which begins at about 6,000 feet (1,829 meters), is limited to high ridges and valleys in the Sierra Nevada de Mérida range. A low, mossy elfin forest grows there, as infertile soils and cold temperatures stunt trees. Most slopes have thin soils. Erosion and landslides have removed much of the topsoil. This area is the "Zone of Grains" because farmers grow wheat and barley in warmer valleys, wherever soils are fertile. Potatoes, protected from damaging frosts by the soil, are also an important crop in this zone. Thus, the potato defines the upper limit of crop production, which is about 10,000 feet (3,048 meters).

The cold and windy environment and poor soils above 10,000 feet (3,048 meters) make farming impossible. Geographers call this subzone the *páramo* ("wasteland"). Precipitation is relatively low, as cloud tops are often below the páramo because of the high elevation. The páramo might be an interesting place to visit, but not a great place to live. Each afternoon, gentle breezes rising from the valleys below bring in a dense fog that blankets the ground. Everything gets wet and cold. Like giant gravestones, rocky crags (steep rugged rocks or cliffs) rise from the stony soil. The chilly climate and poor soil allow only the hardiest grasses and low-lying shrubs to survive. Some of the plants are edible for grazing animals (cattle, sheep, and goats). Livestock raising is the principal economic activity for altitudes up to about 15,000 feet (4,572 meters), above which grasses and other edible plants disappear.

FAUNA

Colombia's wide-ranging habitats result in highly diverse group of animals. In fact, scientists have identified and named 623 species of amphibians, 518 species of reptiles, 467 species of mammals, 3,200 fishes, and a myriad of butterflies and other invertebrates. Moreover, the entire country is a bird-watcher's paradise. It boasts 1,821 species of birds and sits along a major seasonal migratory route for North American birds.

Despite its relatively small area, Colombia is the second-most biologically diverse country in the world. It has more than 1,800 species of birds, including the Yariguies brush-finch, which was discovered in the Andes in 2006.

Like clockwork, a squadron of feathery travelers arrives from that continent to spend their winters in Colombia or to stop there temporarily on their way to destinations farther south. The annual migration includes several species of songbirds and raptors, such as the rose-breasted grosbeak, broad-winged hawk, Swainson's hawk, summer tanager, and others. Because of the dramatic infusion of migratory birds, Colombia is home to roughly 30 percent of the world's known bird species, at least for part of the year.

If you were to visit the Caribbean shoreline and lowlands, you would find a bewildering menagerie of wildlife that depend on mangroves and marshes for resources. These include colorful songbirds, ducks, herons, ibis, crab-eating raccoons, and otters. Among reptiles, the best-represented species is the American crocodile, which is at risk of extinction. A narrow-nose spectacled caiman, green iguana, or boa constrictor might be just a step or two away. You might also see a slow-moving three-toed sloth chewing fresh leaves, otters navigating the streams, and manatees grazing on freshwater plants.

The rainforest is a fairly quiet place most of the time. In the mornings, though, you might hear the male red howler monkey let out a call, which is more like a roar. His call can be heard up to 3 miles (5 kilometers) away. You might also hear the sounds of other howler groups within hearing distance respond. These primates travel in packs of 3 to 16 individuals and avoid conflicts over territory by constantly informing each other of their location. The Santa Marta Mountains are home to many of this and other species. The area also is home to many native birds named after the range, such as the Santa Marta parakeet, Santa Marta wren, Santa Marta brush-finch, and Santa Marta warbler.

There is much to entice a nature lover to the savannas of the northern Oriente, including many North American birds on winter vacation. Dickcissels, which are, perhaps, the prettiest small bird of the North American Great Plains, winter in this subregion. Capybaras—the world's largest rodents—feast on grasses and other plants to keep their compact 110-pound (50-kilogram) bodies well fueled. The wetlands and tree-lined streams of this part of the Oriente are home to roseate spoonbills and other wading birds. Large white-bellied spider monkeys eat fruits and young leaves from trees that grow along river banks. You might see tamanduas, which are tree-dwelling anteaters, using their sticky tongues to snag termites and ants.

Wetter parts of the savanna are also home to the giant anaconda. This dark olive-brown snake often grows to be 13 to 16 feet (4 to 5 meters) long but can grow to more than 30 feet (9 meters) in length. Giant anacondas combine an arboreal life (inhabiting trees) with an aquatic life (inhabiting the water) and are most active at night. They wait for prey while coiled loosely around low-hanging tree branches or submerged in the water with their eyes just above the surface. When capybaras, wading birds, and other animals come to the water's edge, they attack, coil around, and kill their prey by constriction. Then they slowly swallow the dead carcass whole.

Wildlife in the wetter southern Oriente, where there is rainforest, is equally interesting. If you are lucky, you might see a tapir, a large browsing mammal that has a pig-like body with a great tapering nose. Trees provide a habitat for several types of monkeys that forage their canopies for fruits, leaves, nuts, and insects. Night monkeys, as their name implies, are nocturnal (active at night) and use their large eyes for night vision. The white-faced saki is a tree-living, fast-moving, and shy monkey that makes bird-like chirping sounds to communicate. This primate is active during the daytime, as it moves from branch to branch eating fruits, leaves, and insects. Also found in the southern Oriente is the squirrel-sized tamarin monkey, which jumps quickly from branch to branch. Because they live in such large groups (of up to 40 or more), their chatter and movement makes their presence obvious.

Flowering vines and the sweet smell of orchids attract the attention of hummingbirds and butterflies. Below, on the open forest floor, a tortoise might amble along, eating ripe fallen fruits. A jaguar, whose powerful jaws can easily crack a tortoise shell, may be lurking in the bushes nearby. Overhead, hidden among the shaded branches, a zone-tailed hawk may be on the lookout for small prey.

As you travel from the Oriente plains toward the Andes, you might encounter creatures that inhabit the transitional scrub forest, such as the armadillo and giant anteater. Entering the humid forest of the Andes, a mountain lion, spotted cat, or spectacled bear could be warily stalking you. A Colombian tapir or the mountain tapir (a threatened species) may try to flee into the forest. No doubt the spider monkey, the Andean woolly monkey (a threatened species), the yellow-eared parrot (actually on the verge of extinction), and many more animals may be watching you from the tree canopy. If you keep climbing, you will come to the páramo, or alpine grassland, which is home to an unique hummingbird—the bearded helmetcrest— that bird-watchers from throughout the world come to see because it only lives in this region. Unlike most birds, the helmetcrest builds nests in cavities in bare rock because there are no trees in the páramo. Because there are almost no flowering plants, the helmetcrest depends on insects rather than nectar for much of its diet. It has a short bill and somewhat larger legs and feet than other hummingbirds, and it often hunts insects while walking on the ground.

One of the most unique assemblages of animals in South America is in the Chocó region. The tall peaks of the northern Andes mark the area's eastern boundary and act as a formidable barrier between the Chocó and animals that attempt to migrate into it. For this reason, the species found here are quite different from those found on the other side of the mountains. Many are endemic species, meaning they originated in the Chocó region. Indeed, the Chocó is famous for its large number of endemic species of fauna, including the Lita woodpecker and plumbeous forest-falcon. Two other noteworthy birds found in the area are the harpy and black-and-white crowned eagle, both of which are increasingly rare in many tropical areas of the Western Hemisphere. Baird's tapir is not an endemic species, but it is one of the largest of the hundreds of mammal species in the region. It grows to be more than 6 feet (2 meters) long and weighs between 525 and 880 pounds (240 to 400 kilograms).

THREATS TO NATURAL HABITATS AND WILDLIFE

In an attempt to preserve as much of its natural endowment as possible, Colombia has created more than 40 national parks, sanctuaries, and natural reserves. Los Katíos National Park, a

World Heritage site, is in northwestern Colombia. It is home to a number of threatened animal species and many endemic plants. Protected areas are spread across the country, some easily accessible and others so remote that their number of yearly visitors can be counted on two hands. Unfortunately, because the total area of parkland is enormous, safeguarding against illegal settlement and exploitation is difficult.

Each year, Colombia loses nearly 494,211 acres (200,000 hectares) of natural forest, according to figures released by the United Nations in 2003. Many scientists, however, believe that the true figure may be higher, because an estimated 247,105 acres (100,000 hectares) of native forest are illegally cleared every year. The vast majority of this loss is primary forest, which covers more than 80 percent of the country. Deforestation in Colombia results from many activities. Small-scale agricultural activities, logging, mining, and energy development take their toll, as do construction, large-scale agriculture, draining of wetlands, and the cocaine trade.

Colombia's Chocó rainforest is probably the country's most threatened woodland. Gold mining and palm oil plantations are causing its demise. Coca production, which requires the clearing of trees to plant coca bushes, is also expanding in this region. Many of Colombia's birds and other animals are on the endangered or the vulnerable species list because humans destroy their habitats. Killing animal species off for meat and for collection of exotic species for the pet trade are also major threats. Despite these significant setbacks, though, most people of Colombia realize that plants and animals are important resources for the future and want to protect them. This realization is part of Colombia's historical development—the subject of the next chapter.

CHAPTER

3

Colombia Through Time

Geographers and historians look somewhat differently at events throughout the past. To geographers, "history" is a recording of various past processes and events. Basically, they are interested in learning more about anything that has contributed to the formation of Earth's varied places, features, and conditions, both physical and human. Historians, on the other hand, tend to emphasize individuals, events, and dates. In fact, many historians insist that "history" begins with the dawn of writing. Considering that few Amerindians had written languages, they would have no history in this narrow view! Can you imagine trying to understand present-day Latin America without knowledge of its native peoples and their many contributions? In this chapter, you will travel back through the corridors of time in order to better understand Colombia's past and how it helped shape the present.

EARLIEST PEOPLES

The earliest peopling of the Americas remains one of the great question marks in all of human science. Scientists really do not know for sure who the earliest people to reach the New World were, where they came from, how they traveled, or when they arrived. There are, of course, many theories. One theory is that early hunters walked from Asia to present-day Alaska, crossing a then-dry Bering Strait "Land Bridge." (During the ice age, with so much water locked up in glacial ice, sea level was an estimated 400 feet [122 meters] lower than today.) They may have reached the southwestern United States about 12,000 years ago. Today, however, this theory is being challenged. Archaeological evidence from various sites in South America place the earliest humans in the southern continent thousands of years earlier—perhaps even 30,000 years ago.

If the early migrants came by land, they would have passed through the North American continent and first entered Colombia as their journey continued southward. This, of course, suggests that South America's first human inhabitants lived in or passed through Colombia. One problem with this theory is what is called the Darien Gap, an extremely inhospitable stretch of steaming, disease-infested, swamp, marsh, and rainforest in the region where present-day Panama and Colombia join. Even today, there is no road that passes through the area and it has very few inhabitants.

A second theory, and one that is rapidly gaining support among scientists, is a coastal route. With sea level much lower than today, much of the continental shelf would have been exposed above the Pacific. People could have alternately walked and rafted along the coast. A growing body of archaeological evidence supports this hypothesis.

If, indeed, this was the route traveled, the earliest humans still would have crossed through the land that is today Colombia as they journeyed southward. Unfortunately, little if any archaeological evidence exists to support, or to refute, either theory. In fact, because of the hot, wet tropical climate (which

Prehistoric cave paintings such as the ones pictured here in the Llano region of eastern Colombia, near the town of Inírida, reveal that humans have lived in South America for tens of thousands of years. Today, Amerindians still make up more than half of the population of this region of Colombia.

hastens organic decay), dense vegetation, and other factors, few traces of early humans have been found in Colombia. Very little is really known about the country's earliest inhabitants.

NATIVE CULTURES

From the dawn of human settlement to the present day, Amerindians have played a vital role in Colombia's cultural history. Although today they number only about one percent of the country's population, more than half of all Colombians can trace at least part of their ancestry to native roots. The importance of Ameridians to Colombia reaches far beyond population numbers alone, though. Many very important agricultural crops may have been first domesticated and cultivated in Colombia. Colombian arts—music, dance, painting, literature, and other forms of artistic expression—reveal a strong Amerindian influence. Native peoples certainly played an important role in the early Spanish era of exploration, settlement, and colonization.

Anthropologists divide Colombia's native cultures into two basic groups, based on their means of subsistence: simple and advanced farmers. Simple farmers include the Arawak and Carib groups—the latter of which the Spanish believed practiced cannibalism. Scholars remain divided in regard to whether the Caribs actually engaged in this gruesome practice. (In Spanish *caribe* means "savage," or "cannibal," hence, Carib, and Caribbean, or the "Cannibal Sea"!)

These peoples practiced "slash-burn" farming, shifting cultivation within forested environments. Trees and other vegetation were cut, the debris was left to dry, and then it was burned. The ash added some fertility to the soil. Crops were planted using a dibble, a simple pointed digging stick. They included manioc, sweet potatoes, peanuts, and maize (corn) as staple foodstuffs. Also grown were condiments, such as hot peppers, fruits including the pineapple and avocado, indigo (a blue dye), cotton, and tobacco. Because of the heavy rainfall, nutrients are rapidly leached from the soil, which becomes infertile after several years. As a result, fields (and often villages) were shifted from place to place.

Shelters were crude pole and thatch structures, often with a protective roof but open sides. If you have ever rested in a hammock, you have these people to thank, because they were the first to develop this hanging bed. Even today, many native peoples of tropical South America sleep in hammocks. They also made *tapa*, a type of cloth made from the bark of trees. Because their crops lacked protein, hunting and fishing were important sources of this essential nutrient. Many ingenious devices were used to fish; these included traps, nets, spears, and *barbasco* poisoning. The last method uses poisonous plant extracts. Fish are attracted to still water into which an insect nest has been thrown. Barbasco is added and soon the fish float to the surface stunned and immobilized, rather than dead. The author has seen this practice in the Guianas (northeastern South America) and it works. The natives were also skilled hunters and used poison-tipped arrows.

When listing "high civilizations of ancient Latin America," groups such as the Olmec, Mayan, Aztec, and Quechua (Inca) usually come to mind, but the Chibcha (also called Muisca) of Colombia also attained a very high level of culture and social interaction. In South America, in fact, only the Incas had a higher population or were more culturally developed and politically organized. Some 500,000 Chibchas lived in the high mountain valleys surrounding the present-day cities of Bogotá and Tunja. They cultivated many crops, including maize from Mesoamerica, quinoa (a small grain), and potatoes from the Central Andes. The Chibchas were skilled artisans, known for their goldsmithing, weaving, and emerald jewelry.

History, however, perhaps best recognizes the Chibcha for what some scholars believe was one of the greatest "con jobs" of all time. By the time the Spanish reached the interior valleys of Colombia, the Chibchas were well aware of the countless brutal atrocities the Spanish had committed elsewhere in Latin America. They also knew the Spanish thirsted for gold—and thus, the legend of *El Dorado*, the "Gilded One," may have been born. There are many versions of this legend and it is difficult to know which, if any, is to be believed.

One version suggests that when the Spanish conquistadors first reached the Chibcha, they were told of a chieftain who covered himself with gold dust. On a regular basis, he washed the gold from his body and it would fall to and accumulate on the floor of a lake. This supposedly occurred far to the east—which happened to be one of the world's most isolated and difficult environments: the tropical lowlands of the Orinoco Basin. The Chibchas knew that if the Spaniards ventured into the hot, humid, disease-infested lowlands, they would likely never return. Decades later, Sir Walter Raleigh traveled up the Orinoco River in search of El Dorado. Upon his return, he is reported to have said (perhaps paraphrased), "He who travels the Orinoco, either dies or comes back *loco* ["crazy"]."

THE SPANISH *ENTRADA*

Entrada is the Spanish word for "entrance" or "gateway." It is used in reference to the arrival and entry of Spanish conquerors in the New World. Christopher Columbus, of course, arrived in 1492. The Spanish wasted little time in settling and gaining control of all islands in the Caribbean on which gold was found—Cuba, Puerto Rico, Jamaica, and Trinidad. Soon, they turned their attention to *tierra firme,* the mainland. At first, they simply traveled the coastal zone, where early contacts—some hostile, others friendly—were made with various Amerindian groups. By 1525, they had found alluvial gold (in clay or silt, deposited by water) in the vicinity of the present-day city of Santa Marta, the first Spanish settlement in what is now Colombia.

As early as 1503, Spanish sailors had discovered a large, well-sheltered natural harbor that they claimed was comparable to the best in Spain. There, however, they found fierce-fighting natives who tipped their arrows with deadly poison. Faced with such hostilities and the belief that the Amerindians were cannibals, the Spanish queen, Isabella, gave permission to subdue, capture, and sell the natives as slaves. This relationship certainly did not lead to harmony between the two groups! In fact, it was not until 1533—three decades after their discovery of the wonderful harbor—that Cartagena was established. Because of its ideal physical setting and strategic location on the Caribbean, the city soon became Spain's most important port in all of South America. It held this position for many decades.

By the mid-1530s, having successfully conquered the vast and powerful Inca Empire in the Central Andes, the Spanish began to branch out in search of other wealth and peoples to conquer. Gonzalo Jiménez de Quesada was one such Spanish conquistador. He moved northward from Peru with a small group of 166 men and conquered the powerful Chibcha Empire and its estimated 500,000 people. At the site of their capital city, Bacatá, the Spanish established their own seat of government, Bogotá, in 1538. The city soon became one of the most important colonial Spanish political, social, and economic centers in the New World.

SPANISH COLONIAL ERA

By the mid-sixteenth century, Colombia's role in New Spain (as Spanish holdings in the New World were called) expanded. In 1549, Bogotá gained the status of capital of New Granada, an area that included much of present-day Colombia. Nearly two centuries later, in 1739, the city became capital of the newly established Viceroyalty of New Granada. This expanded territory included much of present-day Colombia, Venezuela, Ecuador, and Panama. The move placed Bogotá in the company of Lima, in present-day Peru, and Mexico City as one of Spain's major colonial administrative centers.

Geographers, historians, political scientists, and other scholars have long attempted to explain Latin America's social, economic, and political woes. There is, of course, no single reason for the difficulties. Rather, the problems stem from a considerable number of often extremely complex factors. What follows is a brief overview that focuses on some of the major factors contributing to the region's problems. Many years ago, the author attended a lecture on Latin America in which the speaker repeatedly referred to the "sixteenth-century [Iberian

Spanish explorer Vasco Núñez de Balboa began the conquest of Colombia in 1508, and within the next few decades settlements such as Cartagena became important economic hubs. Much of the city's original architecture has remained intact, including this section of the city near San Pedro Cathedral, which is located in the heart of downtown.

cultural] baggage" that was imposed on Spain's colonies in the New World. Spain, and much of the rest of Europe, was deeply entrenched in a feudal society. A very small percentage of the population held nearly all of the wealth and power. A middle class was all but nonexistent, and the majority of the population was poor and powerless. This system was also imposed on Spain's New World colonies and is a problem that continues even today. People of Spanish ancestry, of course, are those at the top of the socioeconomic scale.

In settling the Spanish realm within the Americas, the colonists' primary goal was to find mineral wealth, particularly gold. Unlike most Europeans, they came as seekers of fortune, rather than permanent settlers. Nearly all the Spanish settlers believed that they would strike it rich and return to Spain—an attitude that does not contribute to continuity and stability. In addition, in a mining economy, there are those (very few) who prosper and there are those who contribute the labor and remain very poor. Once wealth, whether monetarily or in land and other property, is amassed, it tends to perpetuate itself. This reality is expressed in the saying, "The rich get richer and the poor get poorer." This is particularly true in a feudalistic society that lacks a middle class. The wealthy, of course, control the land, most businesses, and the reins of political power. It is extremely difficult to change this pattern once it becomes entrenched.

Farmers worldwide tend to be egalitarian (a condition of social, economic, and political equality), but, again, the Spanish were soldiers of fortune. They had no desire to settle and work the land. In fact, a Spanish *caballero* ("gentleman") avoids manual labor. During the colonial era, the Spanish attempted to enslave Amerindians and, being largely unsuccessful in this endeavor, introduced slaves from Africa. Today, of course, agriculture is extremely important to Colombia's economy. Most farms are owned and operated by mestizos, though, not by those of Spanish descent. These are just some of the problems that Colombia and other Latin American countries have faced through time. Others will be discussed in the chapters on people and culture, economics, and political geography.

For a number of reasons, Colombians, including many with Spanish roots, gradually grew tired of Spain's firm control. A particular problem was the vast wealth generated in New Granada, much of which was sent to Spain. Many Latin Americans complained that there was little capital left over to be used in colonial development. Some idea of the amount of wealth that left the Spanish colonies was detailed in a news item that broke in mid-May 2007. Although many details had not yet been revealed at the time of this writing, an early sailing vessel was discovered on the floor of the Atlantic Ocean. When deep-sea explorers entered its cargo hold, you can imagine their shock and joy when they found that it contained an estimated $500 million worth of gold and silver coins! That treasure was relatively small, however, compared to one found more than two decades earlier. In 1708, a Spanish galleon carrying an estimated $2 billion ($10 billion according to some estimates) worth of gold, silver, and emeralds sank just a few miles from the port of Cartagena. In 1982, a group funded by 100 American investors discovered the wreckage. By international law, ownership is supposed to be "finder's keepers," but the Colombian government immediately claimed that the wreckage was in their territorial waters and, hence, belonged to them. Ownership of the treasure is still pending after several decades of bitter legal and political maneuvering.

By the early nineteenth century, Colombians were ready to openly defy Spanish authority. Simón Bolívar (for whom the country of Bolivia was named) and Francisco de Paula Santander led a long and bitter war for independence from Spain. Ultimately, they were successful and Gran Colombia (present-day Colombia) became independent on July 20, 1810.

Bolívar was the first president, and Santander served as vice president. The fledgling country experienced several turbulent decades, during which territory was expanded and then lost. Ultimately, in 1830, it collapsed entirely, and Venezuela, Ecuador, and New Granada emerged from the debris as independent states. By 1863, New Granada changed its name to the United States of Colombia, and 23 years later, in 1886, it adopted its current name, the Republic of Colombia.

THE REPUBLIC OF COLOMBIA

During the nineteenth and early twentieth centuries, Colombia held free elections and developed a tradition of civilian democratic government. Even so, the country was sharply divided between liberals (who followed the philosophy of Santander) and conservatives (who were influenced by Bolívar). Civilian rule was interrupted on three occasions by military takeover—in 1830, 1854, and 1953 to 1957. The country also experienced two bloody civil wars, sparked by the bitter rivalry between the Liberal and Conservative parties. The first, called "War of a Thousand Days," lasted from 1899 to 1902. An estimated 120,000 people died in this conflict, which left much of the country in ruin. A half-century later, from the late 1940s to the late 1950s, an even more bitter conflict occurred. During *La Violencia* (The Violence), as many as 300,000 people died, and once again, much of the country's infrastructure and economy were destroyed.

Since its creation in 1810, Panama had been a Colombian province. By the dawn of the twentieth century, however, the United States formalized plans to build a canal across the Isthmus of Panama. The U.S. government was deeply concerned that the Colombian government lacked stability. Leaders were worried that conflict in that country could jeopardize this vital project, which would create the long-sought-after water link between the Atlantic and Pacific oceans. In 1903, Panama

gained its independence from Colombia. The massive under-
taking began immediately, and the canal was finally completed
and opened in 1914.

THE TURBULENT LAST HALF CENTURY

The last 50 years have been a time of great turmoil in Colombia. The chaos stems primarily from the rampant narcotics
trade and resulting conflicts. Many factions have been and
continue to be involved. The government, economy, settlement, and society have all been negatively impacted. As a result,
Colombia's image has been tarnished within the global community. With more than one-half million crime-related deaths
since 1980 (nearly 18,000 each year), the country has long
been one of the world's most violent places. The causes and
consequences of Colombia's violence will be discussed at some
length in subsequent chapters. Ultimately, it is the people who
most suffer from such conflicts. In the following chapter you
will come to better know the Colombian people, their demographic (population) conditions, and various aspects of their
culture.

CHAPTER

4

People
and Culture

olombia, as is true of many Latin American countries, exhib-
its a rich blend of Amerindian, Spanish, African, and other
human features. This is true in regard to both biological
ancestry and culture (a people's way of life). Today, in fact, it is this
mix of human traits that best defines Colombia's population and
lifestyle. In this chapter, you will come to better know and understand
Colombia's people. You will learn about their demographic (statistical data pertaining to the human population) characteristics and
patterns of settlement. You also will meet the various ethnic groups
that have created Colombia's unique and somewhat diverse human
landscapes. Finally, the chapter identifies the major culture traits that
bind Colombians together, including their language, religion, society,
and diet.

POPULATION

Colombia took a census of its citizens in 2005, but population figures vary greatly depending on the source. They range from an estimated 43 million to 48 million. The best guess is that it falls somewhere between 44 to 45 million people in 2010. To a statistician, specific numbers might be important. To a geographer, however, it is the "big picture" that is significant. For example, in Latin America, only Brazil (201 million) and Mexico (112 million) have more people. The population of Colombia is also quite young. About 27 percent of all Colombians are under 15 years of age and only about 6 percent are older than 65 (figures for the United States are 20 percent and 13 percent, respectively). The median (middle) age is 27.6 years, compared to 36.8 years in the United States.

Despite the relatively young age of Colombians, their rate of annual population increase is 1.18 percent per year and declining. In fact, it is comparable to the world average of just under 1.2 percent annual gain and has dropped well below the 1.7 percent average for the less-developed world. Another index of anticipated population growth or decline is the total fertility rate. For Colombia, this figure is 2.2, which means that a Colombian woman will give birth to an average 2.5 children during her fertile years. The figure has dropped by more than half during recent decades and is approaching the replacement only level of 2.1. Nonetheless, the country's population is projected to reach 66 million by mid-century. During most of the past decade, Colombia's economic growth has exceeded its population gain. This means that the country is not suffering a condition of "over-population." (Over-population is such a difficult population to define that it is rarely used by geographers and other social scientists.)

A peoples' well-being is of much greater importance than their numbers, distribution, or density. Each year, the United Nations Development Program publishes a *Human Development Report*—the Human Development Index (HDI). The HDI presents a comparative measure of such conditions as life expectancy, literacy, education, and standard of living. In 2009, Colombia ranked seventy-seventh among the 182 countries included in the study. This represents a drop of seven spots from its 2006 position. Among the key criteria rated, the country enjoys a literacy rate of about 93 percent with both males and females being within a fraction of a percentage point of one another. Life expectancy at birth is 74.3 years (71 years for males and 78 years for females), nearly a decade longer than the average among the world's less-developed countries. Most Colombian youngsters have access to public or parochial schools. The per-capita Gross Domestic Product, or the Purchasing Power Parity (GDP-PPP, or buying power in the United States), is $9,200, the eighth highest among all non-Caribbean Latin American countries. One can only imagine what Colombia's HDI rating would be if the country was politically stable!

SETTLEMENT

Settlement refers to where people live—in cities or rural environments, clustered or dispersed, in one or more particular areas of a country, and so forth. Strangely, the most commonly used figure—population density—is also the least important piece of data. It really tells almost nothing about where people actually live. In Colombia, for example, the density is about 100 people per square mile (39 per square kilometer). A population distribution map of the country reveals just how misleading this figure is.

Nearly all Colombians are clustered in the central highlands, in or around Bogotá, or along the northwestern coast around the port city of Barranquilla. Many of these areas have 500 or more people per square mile (200 per square kilometer). On the other hand, in the sparsely populated eastern lowlands, which constitute roughly one-half of the country, the density is fewer than 2 people per square mile (1 per square kilometer).

Another useful figure that helps one better understand a country and its people is rural versus urban settlement. Among the world's less-developed regions, Latin America is somewhat unique. It is 80 percent urbanized, yet relatively poor. Most countries within the region have not yet become fully industrialized. Low-paying primary industries such as farming, mining, and logging often play a greater economic role than do urban manufacturing, sales, and services (a topic discussed in Chapter 6). The result is huge, sprawling cities that are unable to provide their residents with a decent income or standard of living.

This is true of Colombia as well. Approximately 75 percent of the country's people live in cities, with nearly 8 million (about 18 percent of Colombia's total population) in the Bogotá metropolitan area alone. For at least the past half-century, the country has experienced a substantial rural-to-urban migration that has drained the countryside of people. Today, only about 25 percent of all Colombians live in the country or inhabit small rural villages.

As urban ideas and values spread into the country, rural people became increasingly attracted to cities and what they offer. This urban lure and resulting country-to-city migration follows a long-standing worldwide trend. A century ago, most people lived in the country. They subsisted primarily, if not exclusively, on a self-sufficient folk economy. People hunted, fished, gathered, grew, or made nearly everything they needed to get by. What they were unable to provide themselves, they obtained through simple barter, or trade.

With the dawn of industrialization and commercialization, this changed. People began moving to the city in search of jobs. In the city, they became involved in a cash economy. An income was earned for work performed and money was paid for what they needed. In addition, to function successfully in a city, one must be formally educated. Rural knowledge and skills have little value in urban environments. To succeed, one must be able to read, write, and use a variety of mathematical functions. The downside to this migration trend is that many rural environments are drained of their

During the past half-century, Colombians have gradually migrated to the country's urban areas. Today, only about 25 percent of the nation's citizens live in rural areas. Pictured here is a residential area in the village of Bete, which is located on the Atrato River in the northern part of the country.

population. As a result, their potential to further develop the rural economy is lost.

ETHNICITY

For many centuries, people have attempted to classify humankind into various meaningful groups. It has proved largely to be an exercise in futility. Today, such terms as *race, nationality, ethnicity*, and *culture* have lost their meaning (if, indeed, they ever were valid concepts). In this book, *race* is used in reference to one's biological inheritance. *Nationality* refers to one's sense of self-identity or belonging. Basically, it is the answer one gives if asked "What are you?" A Colombian who lived for years in the United States, for example, might still reply to such a question with "Colombian." *Ethnicity*, as used by most American geographers, refers to a minority population.

When the Spanish arrived in Colombia, the country already had a native Amerindian population that may have numbered one to 2 million. Soon after their arrival, African slaves were introduced as laborers on tropical plantations. These three groups constitute the foundation of the country's population. Over time, however, the population became increasingly mixed. Today, only about one-third of the people still identify themselves as belonging to one of the "pure" groups.

"Whites," primarily of Spanish ancestry, but including small numbers of British, French, Lebanese, and others, claim about 20 percent of the population. Afro-Colombians, including *mulattoes* (mixed black and white) and *zambos*, (mixed black and Amerindian), account for another 21 percent of the people. A small one percent of the population claims Amerindian ancestry. An estimated 58 percent of the population is *mestizo*, a mixture of white and Amerindian. Today, as is true throughout much of Andean and Middle America, mestizos are the most dominant and often influential members of society. In Colombia, many mestizos hold high positions in government and the business community.

LANGUAGE

Spanish is the official and almost universal language spoken throughout Colombia. Small numbers of Amerindians, usually those living in very remote locations, continue to speak in their native tongue. Initially, the country's Amerindian population spoke nearly 100 different languages. Today, an estimated 78 are "living" (still spoken) and about 20 have become extinct. The number of native language speakers is diminishing rapidly.

The loss of native tongues (hence, cultures) presents a moral and cultural dilemma. Many individuals and numerous organizations stress the importance of cultural survival among traditional societies. They want these small, often dying cultures to preserve their language and other aspects of their traditional (therefore "primitive") way of life. Their romanticism and desire to know that such people still exist in some remote setting is supported by many in the international community. At the same time, however, such actions can create many ethical problems. Is it fair for culturally well-developed people who live a life of urban comfort to impose their will on others? In essence, if their whim prevails, these small, powerless, remote groups will be destined to short, meager, impoverished lives. They will be economically, politically, and socially marginalized while surviving as living human museum pieces in some wilderness.

RELIGION

When the Spanish conquerors arrived, the region's native peoples practiced many different belief systems. Within decades, Catholic missionaries had introduced their faith to all but the most remote native tribes. The strength of their faith and resulting missionary zeal is illustrated by the fact that, today, an estimated 95 percent of all Colombians claim Catholicism as their faith. Historically, the Church also played a very powerful role in many, if not most, of Colombia's institutions. Its often heavy hand was felt in political, economic, and social realms. It also played a very positive role (in addition to theology) in such areas as health care, education, and serving as a unifying bond for Colombian society. Although the vast majority of Colombians claim to be Roman Catholic, very few actively practice their faith. This situation is widespread throughout

Approximately 95 percent of Colombians consider themselves Catholic, which, until 1991, was Colombia's official religion. Here, church parishioners participate in a procession during a Palm Sunday mass in Bogotá's Ciudad Bolivar district.

Latin America. In fact, one often hears that "a Catholic goes to church three times—to be baptized, to be married, and for his or her funeral."

Until 1991, Roman Catholicism was Colombia's official religion. The revised 1991 constitution, however, granted all Colombians the right to freely practice their religion, regardless of the faith. Today, about 3 percent of the population belongs to various Protestant groups. Another 2 percent, mainly Colombians of African descent, practice faiths that blend forms of spirit worship with Roman Catholicism. During recent decades, various terrorist groups have kidnapped and killed many religious leaders and followers in an attempt to discourage the practice of religion.

SOCIETY

Colombian society, as is true throughout much of Latin America, is highly stratified. The lower socioeconomic class—as measured by income, education, power, and other indices—is occupied by fully 75 percent of the population. Amerindians, Colombians of African descent, and many mestizos fall within this group. At the opposite extreme, the elite upper class includes about 5 percent of the population, nearly all of whom are white and of Spanish descent. In between is a small middle class, perhaps 20 percent of the population, composed primarily of whites and mestizos. This upper 25 percent of the population, however, accounts for an estimated 80 percent of the country's gross national product (GNP). They also hold most positions of power and influence. Nearly all of them live in the country's various cities. The poorest Colombians live in rural areas, small communities, or in urban slums. They are unemployed or underemployed and poor. As a result, they are often undernourished, suffer from poor health, are poorly educated, and have few opportunities to advance themselves socially or economically.

Customs vary greatly. Urban professionals tend to be very formal. Their clothing is conservative; men wear dark suits and women also dress appropriately for the workplace or social events. Particularly in and around Bogotá, people speak slowly, clearly, and grammatically "proper" Spanish. In the country and small villages, life is much more relaxed. Dress is apt to be casual and comfortable, often reflecting local clothing traditions. Language, although Spanish, is more rapidly spoken, slang and local accents are more common, and less attention is given to "correct" delivery. Social interactions also are more formal in Bogotá and the surrounding areas. In the coastal areas and countryside, people tend to be much more open, friendly, and informal. Both patterns are rather typical of those found worldwide, regardless of culture.

Diet and Dining

It is often said that "we are what we eat." To cultural geographers, just the opposite is true: "We eat what we are." That is to say, our culture determines what is eaten, the nature of its ingredients, how food is prepared, and when it is eaten. Culture also provides us with eating utensils and manners, rules on who eats when and with whom, what beverages are consumed, and so forth. Diet, in fact, may be the single most valid and revealing cultural practice in understanding a people.

In Colombia, many factors influence one's diet and dining practices. Afro-Colombians, Amerindians, and Spaniards each eat quite differently. So, too, do affluent, well-educated, upper-class urbanites and rural poor, regardless of heritage. Upper-class families are most apt to parallel the Spanish traditions of Mediterranean Europe. Ingredients may be different than those with which the reader is accustomed, but were you to dine in an upper-class Colombian home, you would feel quite comfortable. (But mind your manners!) Most middle-class people have a diet that blends both Amerindian (or Afro-Colombian) and Spanish practices, both in terms of ingredients and dining customs.

One major difference between Colombian food customs and those most common throughout Northern America is the scheduling of meals in regard to the type and amount of food consumed. Breakfast is normally very light—perhaps nothing more than coffee, juice, fruit, and a roll. The noonday meal is often the largest, similar to the evening meal throughout most of the United States and Canada. It may consist of several courses and take an hour or more to consume. Traditionally, it has been followed by a *siesta*, or nap. Many people believe that the siesta is an adaptation to tropical heat and humidity, but this is not the case. Even today, an after-lunch nap is commonplace throughout much of temperate northern Europe. In the evening, a lighter meal is eaten.

Ingredients vary greatly from region to region and also with income and ethnicity. The poor tend to eat what is locally available, whereas the affluent can buy a variety of items both costly and of widespread origin. Beef, pork, and poultry are all popular, as is a variety of seafood in coastal areas. Maize (corn), beans, squash, potatoes (both "white" and sweet), tomatoes, avocadoes, and hot peppers all were first grown in tropical and subtropical Latin America. Today, they continue to be dietary mainstays.

Many Old World crops, of course, were introduced by the Spaniards, including a preference for wheat flour. Coffee, beer, or *aguardiente* (a potent local hard liquor) are often consumed with meals. Colombians rarely drink tea and unlike many Latin Americans, consume very little wine or milk.

The word *culture* appears in the title of this chapter, but perhaps misleadingly so. Culture, after all, includes all human activity, including government and politics, economic functions, and much more. In the following two chapters, you will learn more about the underlying sources of Colombia's current plight—its government, political conflicts, and critical economic problems. You also will see that a very close link exists between the country's political system and its economic condition.

5

Government and Politics

In many respects, a country is very much like a human being. Both have size and shape, which can be significant. Size and shape alone, however, do not determine strength, cultural development, or other important features. For example, excess weight does not neccessarily strengthen an individual. In Colombia, roughly two-thirds of the territory is remote, sparsely settled, and of little economic importance. Further, although Colombia is somewhat compact, it has three appendages, or "panhandles." Such areas tend to be remote and often lie beyond the realm of effective national control. Such areas can offer a haven to terrorists and others whose activities place them beyond the law. For example, the remote Guajira Peninsula, the finger of land that juts into the Caribbean, is a hotbed of drug smuggling.

Humans and countries both have a "heart." In Colombia, Bogotá fills this function. It is a primate city, which means that it is the country's largest and most important urban center. It is the seat of government and also serves as the country's economic, social, and cultural heart. A diseased heart can cause illness, or even death, however. With rampant kidnappings, murders, and other crimes, Bogotá has become one of the world's most dangerous and troubled cities. Politically, anyone who speaks out or acts against the country's drug cartels places his or her life in serious jeopardy.

Both humans and countries have circulation systems that keep life-sustaining elements flowing. Much of Colombia's infrastructure—particularly its highways and railroads—are inadequate. Generally speaking, they are poorly integrated and poorly maintained. The country also has communication networks such as phone, radio, television, and the Internet. When areas of the body are not sustained by circulation, they wither away, and when the communication service of a country is disrupted, the results can be devastating. Have you ever heard the saying, "All roads lead to Rome"? The phrase points to one of the chief secrets of the Romans' success. They built an excellent network of roadways that linked the far reaches of their empire with Rome. In Colombia, however, various parts of the country are quite isolated from one another. There are very few roads in the eastern half of the country, and most of those are passable only during the dry season. Only two all-weather roads reach the Pacific Coast, leaving much of that region isolated from the rest of the country. For a country to be healthy, it is essential that its entire territory be linked together by a well-integrated transportation network. The same holds true for communications. Because its linkages are poorly integrated, many citizens have a rather poor sense of national identity. They prefer to identify themselves as residents of their own river valley, coastal zone, or some other geographic region, rather than as "Colombians."

Humans and countries both have a brain—that part of the body that ultimately is responsible for all other systems. For a country, this would be the government. Throughout much of its history, Colombia's government has been ineffective. Many politicians, judging from news releases, either are "owned" by drug cartels, or, if they openly oppose criminal activities, find their lives in jeopardy. Graft and other forms of corruption are widespread. Conditions are so bad that some observers believe Colombia's government, like those of Afghanistan and Somalia, may be on the brink of collapse. Finally, severe illness can strike both humans and states, often with devastating results. In Colombia, 50 years of civil unrest has made the country severely ill.

SYSTEM OF GOVERNMENT

Colombia is a democratic constitutional republic. Its current constitution, the latest of many, was adopted on July 5, 1991, and has been amended many times. The country is subdivided into 32 departments, each with its own administrative center, and one capital district, Bogotá. Unlike the United States, however, Colombia is a unitary state in which the central government, rather than the individual subunits, holds most of the power. Like the United States, though, the government is divided into three branches—the Executive, Legislative, and Judicial. It also has two dominant political parties, one liberal and the other conservative. The president is chief of state and head of government. A president and vice president are elected by popular vote to four-year terms and are eligible to hold office for no more than two consecutive terms. The president also seeks advice from a Cabinet. The Legislative branch of government also is closely patterned to that of the United States. It is bicameral (divided into two sections), with both a Senate and House of Representatives. The Senate has 102 seats, and members are elected to four-year terms. The House has 166 members who also are elected to four-year terms.

Colombia's court system differs somewhat from that of the United States. There are four high courts, each with a different area of jurisdiction, or responsibility. The Supreme Court of

Juan Manuel Santos became president of Colombia in August 2010. It is hoped that Santos will continue on the same path as his predecessor, Álvaro Uribe, in lessening political turmoil and cracking down on drug cartels.

Justice is the highest court of criminal law and is responsible for hearing criminal cases. A second court, the Council of State, is concerned with administrative law and ensuring that the country's administrators conduct their roles in a legal manner. The Constitutional Court is responsible for interpreting and defending the constitution, including amendments to the document. Finally, the Superior Judicial Council oversees the civilian judiciary and resolves jurisdictional disputes that may arise between other courts within the system. There also are many lower courts.

A TRADITION OF VIOLENCE

It seems paradoxical that a country with a long tradition of democratic government is also one of Latin America's most politically violent nations. The two dominant political parties have gone to war against one another no fewer than eight times since the country gained its independence in 1810. During these conflicts, hundreds of thousands of people lost their lives and millions of others have been forced to leave their homes. In addition, during times of conflict, both the country's government and economy have been in shambles. Colombia's sad plight is expressed in the following passage:

> [V]iolence included left-wing insurgency and terrorism, right-wing paramilitary activity, and narcoterrorism. . . . In mid-1988 many Colombian academics who studied killings by drug smugglers, guerrillas, death squads, and common criminals believed that the government was losing control over the country's rampaging violence. They noted that even if the guerrillas laid down their arms, violence by narcotics traffickers, death squads, and common criminals would continue unabated.

Unfortunately, the violence has continued until the present day. Recently, the United Nations Educational, Scientific and

Cultural Organization, commonly referred to as UNESCO, called Colombia "a culture built on illegality and force." A May 11, 2007, news item in *The UNESCO Currier*, indicated that "In the absence of a legitimate state [a government in control], guerrillas, paramilitary forces and organized crime have each managed to lay down their law." The article went on to indicate that violence claimed 38,000 lives in 2006 and created 10 times that number of refugees. Clearly, Colombia's long nightmare continues. Who are the "players" in this conflict?

(1) *Left-wing insurgents.* Colombia, as is true of many Latin American countries, has a sharply divided society. There are a small number of very wealthy and powerful people, most of whom are Spanish. The great majority, however, are poor, landless, powerless, and of mixed race. This is the ethnic combination that has contributed to conflict throughout much of Latin America. It was a situation in which left-leaning Marxists (and others) found fertile ground for planting the seeds of rebellion. The left-wing insurgents fall into two major groups: the Revolutionary Armed Forces of Colombia (FARC) and the National Liberation Army (ELN).

(2) *Right-wing paramilitaries.* In order to protect their lives, land, and businesses against left-wing insurgents, Colombia's wealthy hire vigilante groups. So do drug traffickers seeking protection against leftist rebels. During recent decades, these paramilitaries have grown in power far beyond their original purpose. Today, many of these groups are deeply involved in the narcotics trade and other illegal activities. The United Self-Defense Forces of Colombia (AUC) is the primary right-wing paramilitary group.

(3) *Drug cartels.* According to many observers, the real power in Colombia is held by drug lords. Many believe that they also are a major source of the ongoing conflict. According to a United Nations source, drug barons financed the election of President Ernesto Samper during the mid-1990s. Clearly, they have the financial capability to exert a very strong

influence on the country's politicians, and hence, political and judicial systems.

(4) *The government, including military.* Despite massive financial (mainly in the form of military) support from the United States, the government seems powerless to curb the violence or to curb the drug trade.

Ultimately, of course, it is the average Colombian citizen who is caught in the cross fire between hostile factions. Why is Colombia so violent? What are the issues underlying the conflict(s)? And who is involved? As is true of many conflicts, the roots go deep and are extremely tangled. Answers are subject to positions, perceptions, and perspectives and often vary greatly depending on who is offering them. One fact is certain: Although Colombia is located on a distant continent, the United States is very much involved. An estimated 90 percent of the cocaine sold in the United States originates in Colombia. The country also is the chief Western Hemisphere recipient of U.S. foreign aid; it has received more than $3 billion since 2000. In the following section of this chapter, the author will attempt to explain the roots of Colombia's ongoing conflict. His assessment is based on his many years of teaching such courses as Geography of Conflict, Problems of Developing Countries, and Geography of Latin America.

A CYCLE OF FRUSTRATION

Many less-developed countries (LDCs) have a history of conflict. Almost always, the underlying problems are very complex in nature and cannot be answered by a single simple answer. "Overpopulation," "bad government," or "poor economy" are typical of the simplistic explanations commonly presented in the media, by politicians, or even academicians in their respective fields.

Native Heritage

As you learned in Chapter 3, Colombia is sharply divided along ethnic lines. The great majority of people are of mixed

Among the most militant of Colombia's guerrilla organizations is Revolutionary Armed Forces of Colombia (FARC). Since its founding in 1964, the left-wing terrorist group has been responsible for the death of thousands of Colombians. Here, a child rides his bike past the ruins of a house in the northern town of Tierradentro, where 17 police officers and two citizens were killed by the group in November 2006.

racial and cultural heritage. When the Spanish arrived, most of Colombia's native peoples practiced a traditional folk culture and subsistence economy. They were self-governing tribal systems and worshipped their own deities in their own way. With the conquest, a strange and foreign culture was imposed on them. In what rapidly became a two-tiered society, the Spaniards wielded the power, whether social, economic, or political. In a growing cash economy, those who practiced mere subsistence fell far behind. If there is truth to the statement "money is power," they were powerless and became increasingly frustrated. They have never played an important role in the political process although have been extremely disruptive to that process. Most of the left-wing insurgents fall within this group.

European Heritage

Mediterranean Europe does not have a long history of democratic government or political stability. In fact, Spain, itself, has only been democratic and somewhat politically stable for several decades. Colombia (and much of Latin America) still suffers from the "sixteenth-century cultural baggage" introduced by the Spaniards, mentioned earlier. The system includes many elements that hinder the development of a stable democratic government. Two, however, stand out. First, the country has a highly polarized socioeconomic structure. There is no well-developed middle class, with all this implies in terms of human equality (income, social position, political influence, and so forth). Second, given the foregoing condition, a very small power elite largely controls the country, and as a result, the majority population is relatively powerless. Such a situation is bound to be politically disruptive.

Natural Environment

Colombia's natural environment also poses a number of challenges to the government. As you will learn in Chapter 7, mountains divide the country into a number of distinct subregions, each with its own "agenda" and strong sense of self-identity. As a result, it is difficult to develop a strong sense of national identity. Many Colombians have a stronger attachment to their immediate locale than they do to their country. In addition, more than half of the country lies outside the realm

Termed "a culture built on illegality and force" by the United Nations Educational, Scientific and Cultural Organization (UNESCO), Colombia still has a long way to go before it can truly be considered a democracy. Here, a Colombian policeman frisks a voter prior to a presidential election at a polling station in the central Colombian town of Guasca.

of effective national control. That is, linkages are weak and the government exercises little, if any, influence in such outlying regions. This is particularly true of the Oriente, which, for all practical purposes, contributes little to the country's economy and is of little political importance.

Natural Resources
Unlike some Latin American states, Colombia does not have a wealth of natural resources on which the government can

depend for revenue. Small amounts of petroleum, natural gas, coal, and nickel are produced and exported, but their contribution to the country's economy and government is minimal. To understand the importance mineral wealth can have to a country, one need only look to neighboring Venezuela (petroleum), or southward to Chile (copper). Despite a significant area of tropical rainforest, this resource is remote and contributes little to the national economy.

Economic System

When people are financially secure, they generally are supportive of their government. In turn, a stable government is able to support and actively promote economic growth and development for its people. As citizens prosper, they pay taxes that help the government provide services such as education, health, roads and other means of transportation, systems of communication, defense, and so on. If needs for these services are not met, however, people blame and often turn against their government. Because of widespread poverty, many Colombians are unhappy with their government, and because so many are poor, they are unable to provide adequate support for government services through taxation.

The drug trade must be added to this complex mix of factors. Inasmuch as drug trafficking is illegal, it seems likely that Colombia's primary source of revenue is not taxed! In addition, drug lords and others involved in the trade wield tremendous power in the political arena. Their influence permeates governments from local and state to the national level.

Infrastructure

A country's infrastructure—its highways, railroads, pipelines, airways, energy distribution, and communication networks—can be either public or privately funded. Their development, of course, can be enormously costly. In Colombia, the government lacks financial resources to adequately contribute to infrastructure development, and private interests are apt to think twice before investing in a country torn by strife. As a result, the country's infrastructure is in poor condition. Poor transportation linkages, for example, contribute to strong feelings of regional sectionalism. They also contribute to large areas of the country being outside the area of effective national control. Such areas are ideal hideouts for terrorists, guerrillas, and drug-related activities.

Population and Settlement

Colombia's population of approximately 44 million places the country in third place among Latin American states. Its density of about 100 people per square mile (39 per square kilometer) is very close to the world average. Such figures alone, however, are rather meaningless. Numerous other factors must be taken into consideration. For example, nearly two-thirds of all Colombians are economically, socially, and politically marginalized. About 12 percent of the population is unemployed (and many more are underemployed; they work but have an inadequate income). As a result, nearly half of the people live below the poverty line. Humans have the potential to be any country's single most important resource, but their potential to contribute is based on such conditions as health, educational attainment, and individual freedom. The Colombian government has far to go in reaching these goals.

Settlement also presents a serious challenge to governments at both the national and local levels. Colombia ranks second in the world, behind only war-ravaged Sudan, in the number of persons displaced by conflict. During the past decade, an estimated 2 to 3 million people have left the countryside. As refugees, they have flocked to the country's cities in search of a safer environment. In so doing, they deplete the countryside of people, reduce agricultural production, and create a vacuum into which criminal elements can move and thrive. In the cities, the migrants swell urban populations; consequently, there are many more people than jobs and services can accommodate. The result, of course, is huge slums and crime rates that rank among the world's highest.

When most people think about "developed" or "less developed," they think in economic terms. As you have seen, many factors influence a country's economic development and closely related human development and well-being. The following chapter presents an overview and analysis of Colombia's economic geography.

CHAPTER

6

Colombia's Economy

By most measures, Colombia falls with that group of countries labeled "less developed." Many of the country's statistics warrant this designation. As many as 100 different criteria must be considered in determining a country's ranking among the world's more than 220 nations. Such figures as per-capita income ($8,205 in 2008) and per-capita Gross Domestic Product ($9,200 in 2009) place Colombia approximately in the middle of the world's countries; so do the number of physicians, literacy rates, and energy consumption. Perhaps the single most valid indicator of a country's position among others is the Human Development Index (HDI). This ranking, which includes a number of important indices, places Colombia at a surprisingly high position—seventy-seventh among the 182 countries rated in 2009. Clearly, Colombia is in a transitional position. Were it to achieve political stability, the country has the potential to join the world's developed nations.

THE DATA

Economists and economic geographers love statistical data. For example, Colombia's Gross Domestic Product (GDP)—the annual value of goods and services produced—is estimated to be $402 billion (in 2009). This figure, alone, however, is rather meaningless. It becomes significant when you know that Colombia ranks twenty-eighth of the world's 226 ranked countries, or that in Latin America, only Brazil, Mexico, and Argentina have a higher total GDP. By 2010, Colombia's economy was already in decline, dropping by 0.10 percent in 2009. Even though it suffered hard times, the country remained in the top 20 percent of Latin American nations in economic "growth" (which is hardly a reason to rejoice). The figure becomes even less significant when one realizes that much of the gain is eaten away by inflation, running at 4.2 percent in 2009. The unemployment rate is 12 percent, not bad by LDC standards. A whopping 47 percent of the population lives below the poverty line, however. This suggests that the rate of underemployment—people working, but not in adequately paying jobs—is huge. Further, the distribution of wealth is cause for alarm. The poorest 10 percent of the population possess less than one percent of the nation's capital, whereas the wealthiest 10 percent controls about 45 percent of the country's wealth.

THE HUGE "GORILLA" ON COLOMBIA'S BACK

For Colombia, most countrywide economic data are meaningless. The illegal trade in narcotics is a huge economic "gorilla" that casts doubt on all economic figures. Although there are many estimates, it is all but impossible to find and present reliable data pertaining to the economic impact of the drug trade. In 2006, U.S. government data suggested that as much as 500 metric tons (551 tons) of cocaine and 6 metric tons (6.6 tons) of heroin were exported from the country annually. The street value of the cocaine alone in the United States was an estimated $67 billion. Some economists placed the annual value of illegal narcotics to Colombia's economy at about $90 billion a year, or

Although the government has had some success curbing the Colombian drug trade, the country still produces between 70 and 80 percent of the world's supply of cocaine. Here, a narcotics policeman organizes 3.1 tons (2.8 metric tons) of cocaine seized at the port of Buenaventura, Colombia.

nearly 25 percent of the country's total GDP at the time. Other estimates, however, are much lower—in the range of 3 percent to 15 percent. Inasmuch as drug lords do not pay taxes on their earnings or file income reports, all drug-related economic data are, at best, guesses.

By 2005, Colombia was believed to produce 80 percent of all cocaine distributed worldwide. The trade employed several hundred thousand people, ranging from farmers to law enforcement officers, judges, and politicians. An estimated $100 million was spent each year on bribes to Colombian officials, causing some observers to call the country the world's first "Narco-Democracy." The drug trade permeated every sector of Colombia's government, economy, and society. It had become one of the most lawless lands in the world, with astronomical rates of murder, kidnapping, and other crimes. The legal economy was devastated. Tourism, for example, which holds vast potential for growth, was all but nonexistent. Few people will vacation in a place where their life is in jeopardy! Thousands of farmers, who could have grown legal crops, such as coffee, turned instead to raising coca and heroin poppies.

The drug cartels hold an awesome amount of power in Colombia. Throughout much of the country, their word was (and in many places continues to be) the "law." During recent decades, to take a stand against their authority could be an honorable, but often fatal, position. Most Colombians were intimidated and lived their lives in constant fear.

Fortunately for Colombia and Colombians, the drug tide is beginning to turn. The United States has been actively involved in helping Colombia curb its drug problem. From 1997 to 2010, more than $5 billion in foreign aid went to the country, most of which was earmarked to fight the illegal drug industry. President Uribe, who held office from 2004 to 2010, made a strong fight against corruption, crime, terrorism, and the drug trade a centerpiece of his administration. His efforts were quite successful. By 2010, each of the areas had experienced a substantial decline. Hopefully, this positive trend will continue during the administration of President Juan Manuel Santos.

It is very easy to blame Colombia and Colombians for their role in this sordid business, which takes a huge toll on people's lives and health. Where does the fault really lie, though? You must remember—not one cent would be made in the production and sale of illegal drugs if no market existed in the United States, Canada, and elsewhere. Is the fault really theirs, or that of people who ruin their lives through the purchase and use of drugs?

PRIMARY INDUSTRIES

Economic activities can be categorized in a number of ways. Many geographers prefer a three-sector classification: primary, secondary, and tertiary. This system will be used in the following discussion of the Colombian economy. Primary industries are those that are based on the direct human use, or extraction, of natural resources. They include agriculture, mining, forestry, and fishing. About 18 percent of Colombia's labor force is engaged in primary economic activities, yet they contribute only about 10 percent of the country's GDP. These figures suggest that the primary industries—agriculture, mining, logging, and fishing—are no longer very important to the country's overall economic growth and development. Of course, one must remember that coca and heroin poppies are agricultural crops, hence, a primary industry.

Agriculture

About 2 percent of Colombia's land is suited for agriculture. Throughout much of the country's history, the raising of crops and livestock was Colombia's primary economic activity. Until well into the twentieth century, most residents were subsistence farmers, engaged in a traditional folk culture and economy. They were mainly self-sufficient, producing, building, or making nearly all of their possessions. What they could not provide for themselves was gained through barter. Their efforts, of course, were not recorded in economic figures such as per-capita income or GDP.

Commercial agriculture began on a very small scale soon after the Spanish arrived, but it grew quite slowly in importance. During the nineteenth century, some sugarcane, tobacco, indigo, and cacao were grown commercially, and much of it went to Spain. Today, some bananas are still exported. You are most apt to find an important Colombian agricultural export (other than coffee) by visiting a florist. Cut flowers are an important export. Colombia offers a moist tropical climate in which flowers can be grown year-round. As you can imagine, exporting this precious and highly perishable cargo received a huge boost about 50 years ago with the beginning of the refrigeration and jet aircraft. Cut flowers can now be whisked from field to market in a day or two.

First introduced to Colombia in the early 1800s, coffee quickly became the country's chief source of legal foreign income. Today, Colombia ranks second in the world behind Brazil in the production of coffee, contributing approximately 12 percent of the world's supply. Here, a boy picks coffee beans in a field near the western town of La Morelia.

By the 1880s, coffee emerged as Colombia's most important (legal) agricultural commodity, and by 1900 it had become the country's chief source of foreign income. Today, the crop continues to contribute about 15 percent of the country's total (legal) export revenue. Colombia produces about 12 percent of the world's coffee, ranking the country in second place behind Brazil. About 500,000 farmers, or approximately 20 percent of the country's agricultural labor force, are engaged in coffee production.

Colombian coffee is widely recognized as being among the world's finest. The country's specialty coffees, in particular, have a splendid reputation for excellence.

These coffees carry a label identifying the variety of bean, the elevation at which the beans were grown, and—as is the case with good wine—the area of the country from which it came. The latter category is important because the quality of coffee beans varies greatly. Such elements as soil type, slope, shade, and moisture can greatly affect bean quality. Just as with wine, true coffee connoisseurs judge the beans (hence, brew) on the basis of several factors. In addition to taste, they recognize such differences as body, aroma, acidity, and fragrance.

"Mountain grown" is a key phrase used in marketing Colombian coffee. Since 1959, a fictitious *cafetero* (coffee farmer) named Juan Valdez has represented the National Federation of Coffee Growers of Colombia in promoting their product. The best varieties come from *fincas* (small farms that specialize in coffee growing) located in mountain valleys, where trees offer constant shade for the coffee shrubs. There, the *cafeteros* tend their precious, highly labor-intensive, crop. Coffee shrubs are carefully tended throughout the year. When ripe, beans are picked by hand, then carefully sorted and washed, and finally spread out on a clean surface to be dried by sun and wind.

Mineral Extraction

From the period of their earliest settlement (Do you remember El Dorado?), the Spanish thirsted for gold. Colombia did not disappoint them. During the eighteenth and nineteenth centuries, the country was one of the world's leading producers of the precious metal. In fact, during much of the first half of the nineteenth century, gold was the country's primary export product. Small amounts of gold, silver, and platinum continue to be mined at various centers scattered throughout the country. In the jewelry industry, it is a rare green gemstone for which Colombia is best known today. For the past half-century, the country has been the world's leading producer of emeralds. In fact, about 80 percent of the highest quality emeralds sold worldwide and 60 percent of the total world yield comes from

Colombian mines. The country also produces and exports substantial amounts of nickel, an alloy metal best recognized in the nickname for the 5-cent U.S. coin (which is 75 percent copper). Columbia also has small deposits of iron ore.

Possessing adequate energy sources is essential to any county's economic growth and cultural development. Colombia is fortunate in that it has adequate supplies of mineral fuels and excellent hydroelectric potential. In the latter context (think of water as a mineral), it ranks second in all of Latin America. If harnessed, Colombia could be a leader in clean, inexpensive, hydroelectric energy. The country has numerous streams, with a reliable year-round flow, that plunge from high elevations. In order to be dammed (harnessed), however, a stream must flow through a deep enough valley or gorge for a dam to be keyed (secured) on both sides. This type of land feature is widespread throughout much of the western half of the country.

Although not a major producer by global standards, Colombia is one of the few countries in all of Latin America that is self-sufficient in energy resources. It shares with Brazil the distinction of having the largest coal reserves in all of Latin America. Production is centered in the Guajira Peninsula. Most of the coal is bituminous, having less than one percent sulfur content, which makes it fairly clean burning. Production, much of which is exported, has doubled during recent years. With more than 7 billion tons (more than 6 billion metric tons) of proven reserves, coal will be an important Colombian export for decades to come. The country also has petroleum and natural gas deposits. It ranks fifth among South American countries in proven oil reserves. Most production comes from the eastern Andean foothills or the eastern lowlands. About half of the oil is exported, most of it to the United States. Production has declined since 1999, but Colombians are optimistic that once the civil conflict ceases, new deposits will be discovered and brought into production. The country also has large supplies of natural gas, an energy source in which it is self-sufficient.

Logging

As you would expect in a tropical land, much of Colombia was initially forest-covered. Centuries of cutting trees for domestic use and to clear land for farming have taken a severe toll on the country's woodlands. Commercial logging, however, is of minor importance to the country's economy. Most of the forested areas are in the eastern lowlands, which has a small population and poorly developed transportation linkages. Further, of the some 1,000 varieties of trees that grow in Colombia, only about 30 are commercially valuable. Those that are most prized are tropical hardwoods such as mahogany. In the tropics, trees do not grow in solid stands and, hence, are widely scattered and difficult to find in the dense rainforest. Also, as hardwoods, they do not float. In the absence of roads, it is difficult to transport cut timber to a saw or pulp mill. Only recently has replanting of deforested areas become common practice. Tropical lowlands may be planted with solid stands of fast-growing species that yield wood for the pulp and paper industries. Deforested Andean slopes are being replanted with commercially valuable pines.

Fishing

Fishing is a poorly developed, yet growing industry in Colombia. Despite bordering on two oceans, most of the catch comes from freshwater inland sources. Domestic production cannot meet the local demand. Commercial species include tuna, sardines, shrimp, and oysters. The industry does hold some promise, and the government is improving fishing industry-related facilities at Buenaventura, the country's largest Pacific port. As a result, the catch has increased greatly during the past two decades.

SECONDARY INDUSTRIES

Secondary industries include manufacturing and construction. Basically, they include the factories or other industries that use or process the raw materials provided by the primary sector.

Despite its numerous rivers and its proximity to both the Pacific Ocean and Caribbean Sea, Colombia's fishing industry has been slow to develop. Today, the industry produces less than 1 percent of the country's gross national product, but the government has targeted the port of Buenaventura as a potential center for development. Here, a boy places fish in the sun on a dock at Buenaventura.

This can be extremely important to a country's economy. Many LDCs export the products derived from their primary industries. A country shipping iron ore or petroleum to some other country for smelting or refining is an example. If a country processes its own natural resources, there is value added to the original resource. Steel and gasoline are more valuable than iron ore and oil direct from the ground. Some Colombian industries are engaged in value-added manufacturing. These include steel mills, several oil refineries, textile mills, fish processing plants, and lumber mills.

These industries, in turn, provide the raw materials used in the manufacture of metal products, petroleum and chemical products, the garment industry, and the wood products industries, including lumber, pulp, and paper. In addition to textiles, agriculture provides the raw materials for food and beverage industries. Finally, in various combinations, the aforementioned products are used in the manufacturing of items ranging from electrical equipment to pharmaceuticals.

For several reasons, manufacturing industries have been slow to develop in Colombia. At times, some businesses have been under public (government) ownership. Rarely is this arrangement in the best interest of a nation's economic development. In addition, for nearly a century, the country's manufacturing economy has faced many problems. Some, such as the Great Depression and World War II, were imposed by forces over which the country had no control. Within Colombia, however, seemingly constant internal conflict, inept governments, widespread corruption, bureaucratic red tape, a poor infrastructure, and a host of other problems have discouraged investment. This is true whether it pertains to Colombians investing in the future of their own country or potential foreign investors. Simply stated, people want to invest in a business environment that is safe and in which their capital resources can grow. This has not been the case in Colombia. Today, secondary industries only contribute about 38 percent of the country's GDP and involve about 19 percent of the labor force.

TERTIARY INDUSTRIES

Tertiary industries are those that provide or produce some service for consumers. They include many businesses, including financial institutions and sales, education, health, transportation, communication, and entertainment. The more developed a country is economically, the higher the percentage of its economy that results from the provision of services. In Colombia, a little more than half of the country's GDP (53 percent in 2009) is generated by tertiary industries that involve about 63 percent of the total labor force. By comparison, in the United States and Canada, 71 percent and 77 percent of the GDP, respectively, comes from service-related industries. They engage more than three-fourth of each country's labor force.

Sales, secretarial work, insurance, restaurants, and so forth differ little in Colombia from those found throughout most of Latin America. Education is the key to socioeconomic development for people in any country, whether developed or less developed. This is particularly true as countries become increasingly involved in the rapidly expanding global post-industrial (service- and information-related) economy. Colombia spends about 5 percent of its entire gross domestic product on education, one of the highest rates in all of Latin America. About 80 percent of Colombian youngsters enter school—nearly 90 percent of them finish the elementary grades (5 years). Just a little more than half of these students go on to secondary school. Approximately 93 percent of all Colombians, both male and female, are literate. Figures are much higher in cities and considerably lower in rural areas. The country also has approximately 150 universities and technical schools. Throughout much of the country's history, the Roman Catholic Church played a key role in providing education at all levels. Today, whereas there are still many parochial schools, the government is assuming a much greater responsibility for public education than in the past.

TRANSPORTATION AND COMMUNICATION

Colombia's transportation network is poorly developed and relatively inadequate. Physical conditions, including rugged terrain and countless broad rivers, make the construction of surface linkages extremely difficult and very costly. Many areas of the country are difficult if not impossible to reach by road or rail. In the late nineteenth century, it was reported that the trip from Bogotá to the Magdalena River (about 100 miles, or

160 kilometers) took as long as an Atlantic crossing by ship! As recently as a half-century ago, surface travel between Bogotá and Cartagena could take up to two weeks. The Magdalena River is navigable to river steamers for several hundred miles. It forms a huge barrier to east-west travel, though, because no bridge spans the huge river for a distance of about 700 miles (1,126 kilometers). Colombia simply lacks the financial resources to construct a well-integrated transportation network.

Even today, it can take days if not weeks to travel between various cities and regions within the country. There are approximately 102,065 miles (164,257 kilometers) of roads, but only about 15 percent of which are paved. The situation with railroads is even worse. Some 2,362 miles (3,802 kilometers) of track is divided by several gauges (width between tracks). One means of travel that is well developed in Colombia is by air. In fact, the national airline, Avianca, has flown commercial routes since 1919. It is the world's second-oldest carrier after the Dutch KLM and the third-largest airline in Latin America. The country has nearly 1,000 airports, at least 35 of which can accommodate large commercial aircraft. Large sections of Colombia, particularly in the Llanos (eastern lowlands), are accessible only by air. In addition to scheduled carriers, many "bush pilots" provide charter service to remote areas.

Communications are fairly well-developed in Colombia. Cellular phones are very popular. In fact, there are nearly seven times as many of them as there are traditional line phones! With more than 41 million in use (2008), there is nearly one cell phone for every person in the country. Approximately 17 million people are Internet users. More than 500 radio and 60 television stations provide service to most of the population.

COLOMBIA AND THE GLOBAL ECONOMY

Colombia must play catch-up in its attempt to become a major player in the rapidly expanding global economy. Other than coffee, can you find any item in your home that is from

Colombia? The odds are that you cannot. Most of the country's exports have been and continue to be natural resources and raw materials produced by its primary industries. For example, its mineral exports include coal, petroleum, nickel, gold, and emeralds. Coffee, sugar, bananas, and flowers are exported agricultural products (as are, of course, undocumented cocaine and heroin). Most exports go to the United States (38 percent), neighboring Venezuela (16 percent) and Ecuador (4 percent).

Because Colombia's manufacturing sector is poorly developed, the country must depend on imports for many necessities. For example, it imports a considerable amount of machinery, transportation equipment, equipment for the oil and gas industry, and aircraft. The country also must import many consumer goods, fuel and electricity, and industrial items such as chemicals and paper products. Major import trading partners include the United States (29 percent), China (12 percent), Mexico (8 percent), and Brazil (5 percent). Fortunately, during recent years, the country has had a positive balance of trade. In 2009, exports amounted to about $34 billion and imports to around $31.5 billion, leaving a balance of $2.5 billion. During recent years, Colombia's economy has shown signs of growth. The government has played an important role in this development. It has attempted to reduce public debt, not spend extravagantly, and improve national security. Further, steps have been taken to increase exports, including signing a free trade agreement with the United States. For the first time in a long time, Colombians can look to their country's economic future with some sense of optimism.

7

Regions
of Colombia

R egions are the geographer's organizational "convenience
packages." For any country, many different criteria can be
used to divide the land into meaningful subdivisions. For
example, landform areas, climatic zones, ecosystems, land use and
economic activity, and population distribution and settlement can be
used for this purpose; so could the country's 32 political administrative units plus the one capital district. In the case of Colombia, one
might even argue that vertical zones would make good sense as the
basis for regional divisions! After all, elevations coincide quite well
with land-use practices throughout the country.

In this chapter, several criteria were used in selecting subregions.
Colombia, to a greater degree than is true of most Latin American
countries, is sharply divided into distinct regions by barriers created
by landforms (for example, mountains). Each region also tends to
have at least one major urban area where most of the population has

settled and also serves as its center of social and cultural activity. In addition, distinct land-use patterns and other economic activities also tend to be associated with each subregion. On this basis, eight regions are identified and discussed in some detail.

CARIBBEAN COASTAL LOWLANDS

The lowland plain facing the Caribbean is Colombia's primary window to the world. It also was the first area of the country to experience European exploration and settlement. Here, most of the population has settled in the three major port cities: Cartagena, Barranquilla, and Santa Marta. The most heavily populated portion of the region occupies the alluvial plain built from deposits of the Magdalena River. Actually, four rivers cross the area, leaving not only fertile deposits of silt, but also a maze of oxbow lakes (formed from a bend in a river), reed-filled marshes, swamps, and stream channels. Until recently, the Magdalena's mouth was so clogged with sand that large vessels could not navigate between the river and the Caribbean Sea. Today, however, passage is possible through a dredged channel. Finally, much of the area is flooded during the April to September wet season.

Cartagena is located on an excellent natural harbor. The city of nearly one million people was founded in 1533 as Spain's primary port on South America's Caribbean coast. As a result, it was one of the major Spanish settlements in the Americas during the sixteenth century. Because of its coastal location and fascinating history, the city is a popular tourist destination. It also is Colombia's second-ranking seaport (behind Barranquilla) and a regional economic center. A good portion of the country's coffee is trucked to Cartagena and shipped from there to world markets.

Barranquilla, a modern industrial and port city, is located on the Caribbean at the mouth of the Magdalena River. Because of its strategic position, the city grew as an *entrepot*, or important trading center. Cargo transported by either river

Located in Cartagena, the fort of San Felipe de Barajas was built by the Spanish in the seventeenth century to defend the coastal city from attack. Today, the fort is a popular tourist destination and a UNESCO World Heritage Site.

steamers or ocean-going cargo ships had to unload when they reached Barranquilla. Warehouses sprouted around the wharves, as did many large import and export businesses. To further encourage commerce, the district was made a free trade zone in which commodities are marketed without paying tariffs or taxes. Today, Barranquilla is a thriving city with a metropolitan population of approximately 2.2 million. In fact, it is the largest seaport, industrial complex, and population center facing the entire Caribbean basin. Because of its function as a port, the city is Colombia's most cosmopolitan urban center. Racially, ethnically, and culturally—in dress, accent, food, and customs—the city differs greatly from the rest of Colombia.

The easternmost of the three major cities occupying Colombia's Caribbean coastal lowland is Santa Marta. Founded in 1525, it is the oldest European-settled community in Colombia and the second oldest in all of South America (Cumaná, Venezuela, was settled in 1521). Steeped in history and sandwiched between the tropical sea and high mountains, Santa Marta has become a major tourist destination. In fact, the city of some 300,000 people has earned a special constitutional designation as a "Tourism, Cultural, and Historical District."

HIGH BASINS OF THE CORDILLERA ORIENTAL

Within the easternmost of Colombia's Andean ranges are several large basins. Despite their high elevations (about 8,000 to 10,000 feet, or 2,400 to 3,050 meters), this is the country's most densely populated area. The Spanish found few minerals in the area, but they did find fertile soils and at these tropical latitudes, a climate favorable for farming. The regional economy developed on the basis of productive agriculture and the importance of the country's capital city, Bogotá. Crops include barley, wheat, and potatoes, as well as a variety of vegetables. In addition, livestock are grazed up to about 11,000 feet (3,350 meters) in this region.

The modern city of Bogotá was founded by the Spanish in 1538, but the area had long been home to the Chibcha civilization. The city lies in a basin 8,661 feet (2,640 meters) above sea level. Although Bogotá is located near the equator, at this elevation its annual average temperature is about 59°F (15°C), the same as Chattanooga, Tennessee. In Bogotá, however, only 2°F (1°C) separate the coldest and warmest months. In Chattanooga, on the other hand, residents experience about a 36°F (19°C) range in January and July temperature averages.

Today, Bogotá and the communities surround it have a total population approaching 8 million. Not only is the city Colombia's major population center, but it is also the country's political, economic, educational, and cultural heart. Economically, Bogotá is home to many corporations, as well as to Colombia's stock exchange and to the offices of most foreign firms conducting business in the country. It also is a major import and export center. Culturally, as you would expect for a capital city of this size, Bogotá is very cosmopolitan. In fact, its nickname is the "Athens of Latin America." Most of its people are of European origin, it is a center of learning and the arts, and its rich history is reflected in its beautiful architecture. Unfortunately, during recent decades, Bogotá's image has become tarnished. By the 1990s, the city had the world's highest rate of murder and kidnapping. Today, however, crime has dropped sharply, and the city actually is safer than a number of U.S. urban centers.

A number of smaller cities dot the landscape of the region's high basins. Much of the economic activity remains primarily agricultural, and there are still a number of subsistence farmers. One major exception is the Paz del Río steel mill near Sogamoso, about 125 miles (200 kilometers) north of the capital. The plant is somewhat unique. All of the raw materials needed to manufacture steel are located nearby. Iron ore, limestone, coal, and an adequate water supply are all found within a radius of about 20 miles (32 kilometers).

LOWER VALLEYS IN THE CORDILLERA ORIENTAL

This region is made up of valleys at elevations below 7,000 feet (2,135 meters), including the valley of the Magdalena River to the west. When the Spanish arrived in Colombia, the region was thinly populated by scattered groups of Amerindians who eked out a meager living from farming, fishing, and hunting. There was little mineral wealth to attract Spanish settlers. Further, conditions were not suited to the growing of tropical plantation crops such as sugar, cotton, and cacao. It was not until the latter half of the nineteenth century that Europeans began to settle this region of mountains and valleys. A startling exchange of crops was about to occur, one that would transform the economy of two lands located half-a-world apart.

Since the seventeenth century, quinine had been used in the treatment of malaria, the world's most prevalent deadly disease. The drug is extracted from the bark of the cinchona tree, which, until the mid-1940s, was the sole source of lifesaving quinine. Cinchona grew wild in the highland forests located in this region of Colombia. Beginning in the mid-nineteenth century, bark was stripped from the trees, collected, and shipped to markets. The city of Bucaramanga was a primary center for this activity. Stripping of bark, of course, killed the trees, which resulted in considerable environmental damage. By the late 1880s, however, plantations on the distant island of Java (Indonesia) had cornered the cinchona-growing and quinine-producing market. Colombia was unable to compete, and the industry there began a sharp decline. Colombia was on the brink of an exchange that would bring sweet revenge, however!

Have you ever heard *Java* used as slang for "coffee"? Originally cultivated in Southwest Asia, coffee shrubs thrived on Indonesian plantations, particularly on the island of Java. By the mid-1800s, however, coffee had been introduced as a commercial crop in Colombia. The exchange more than compensated for the loss of cinchona, because coffee rapidly became Colombia's chief export. Today, it is grown on hundreds of small, mountainside *fincas* (coffee farms), many of which are owner-operated. Within this region, Bucaramanga continues to be a major center of the coffee trade. Other crops, such as tobacco (and, of course, illegal coca, the source of cocaine) have grown in importance during recent decades, as has livestock grazing. The city, the largest in the region, has a metropolitan population approaching one million. In addition to serving as a regional agricultural center, it also provides important political, cultural, and general services functions for the surrounding area. Manufacturing has lagged because surface transportation to and from the city is extremely difficult over the area's rugged terrain.

The broad valley of the Magdalena River is sandwiched between the Cordillera Central and Cordillera Oriental. Surprisingly, perhaps, despite the fertile alluvial soils, the valley supports a rather low rural population density and has few cities of any size. Until the mid-twentieth century, when effective pesticides became readily available, the hot, humid valley hosted swarms of disease-carrying mosquitoes and other insects. In addition, as is the case with the broad flood plain of the Amazon, seasonal flooding that stretches miles beyond the river itself is commonplace. Barrancabermeja, with a population of about 300,000, is the largest city in the valley upstream from Barranquilla. With many oil fields in the area, Colombia's largest oil refinery is located in the city.

THE ANTIOQUIA REGION

The Antioquia Region sits between the valleys of the Cauca and Magdalena rivers and is dominated by the rugged high-mountain and deep-valley terrain of the Cordillera Central. This is a region of active volcanic activity. Mount Tolima, which rises to 17,110 feet (5,215 meters), erupted in 1829 and spread fertile volcanic ash over a large area. In recent times, Nevado del Ruiz erupted violently in 1985, killing 23,000 people and destroying four villages.

The region was first settled by the Spanish, who founded the town of Santa Fe de Antioquia in 1541. The settlement was located near the Cauca River and was surrounded by placer mines that extracted gold from stream gravel. Today, the community that contributed its name to the region is a sleepy and relatively poor town of approximately 23,000 people. Because of the region's terrain, which features high mountains and steep and narrow valleys, Antioquia developed very slowly, both in population and economic activity. In fact, it was not

First colonized by the Spanish in the 1530's, the central Colombian region of Antioquia is home to the bustling city of Medellín. Today an important regional economic center, Medellín is Colombia's second-largest city, with a population of 2.4 million people. Here, residents pass by Colombian artist Fernando Botero's sculpture "Cabeza," which is located outside the Antioquia Museum of Art.

until the mid-1950s that a highway linked the area and Cartagena, on the Caribbean coast. Because of its isolation, Antioquia and its residents, called Antioqueños, remained relatively self-sufficient and very cohesive. They stand apart from other Colombians in a number of ways.

Long a remote, sleepy, economic backwater, Antioquia did not really begin to boom until the early decades of the twentieth century. By 1920, small farmers began to raise coffee, which soon became the dominant crop throughout the area. Transportation linkages were improved, providing easier access to other areas of the country. By 1940, Medellín had become the country's major industrial center, a position it held for several decades. Today, the city is a vibrant urban center of some 2.4 million people. It is Colombia's second-largest city and also the second-ranking economic center. Many national and international companies have headquarters or regional offices in the city.

Industries include steel milling, textile manufacturing, and food and beverage processing, as well as the production of cement, chemicals, and pharmaceuticals. Oil refineries are common. Agricultural production is still very important to the area, and coffee and cut flowers are major exports. The region also is a major producer of coca.

During recent decades, however, the area has gained widespread notoriety of an undesirable nature. You may have heard of the Medellín Cartel, which was perhaps the world's most powerful international drug trafficking organization. Medellín also was a focal point for the violence that hampered the entire country for decades. To add to the city's misery, in the early 1990s, it logged an astronomical murder rate that reached about 9,000 killings a year. During recent years, however, the homicide rate has dropped to around 25 per 100,000, which makes it much safer than many American cities. The drop is attributed mainly to a reduction in gang-related activity.

THE CAUCA VALLEY

Lying between the Cordillera Central and the Cordillera Occidental (Western Range) is a huge structural valley drained by the Cauca River. The valley stretches from Ecuador northward to the Caribbean. The Cauca River, itself, begins near Popayán and flows almost straight, northward, until it joins the Magdalena, near its mouth. Through much of its course, the river flows through relatively soft volcanic ash. As a result, it has eroded deep valleys with steep escarpments (slopes). Most communities, including Popayán and Cali, are built on relatively flat terraces, hundreds of feet above the river itself.

The Spanish entered the Cauca Valley from both the south (Peru and Ecuador) and the north (Caribbean coastal settlements). They found an environment that was well-suited to the growing of sugarcane, a labor-intensive cash crop of great economic value. Finding few Amerindians to work the fields, the Europeans turned to African slave labor. When Colombia abolished slavery in the mid-1800s, the sugar economy fell into sharp decline. For a time, it was replaced by tobacco, cacao, general food crops, and cattle. Today, sugarcane is once again the leading (legal) cash crop in the Cauca valley. Soil, moisture, and temperature conditions are ideal and contribute to some of the world's highest yields. A by-product, bagasse—what is left after the juice is extracted from the sugarcane stalk—is used in a thriving pulp and paper industry. During *La Violencia*, which greatly affected residents who lived in the Cauca valley, more than 200,000 residents lost their lives.

The two primary urban centers in the Cauca Valley are Popayán and Cali. Popayán is the southernmost city in the region. With a metropolitan area population of approximately 260,000 people, it is the smaller of the two urban centers. The city is one of Colombia's most "European" places. It is nick-named the "White City" because of its many old and stately white colonial structures. It has a rich colonial heritage and is the home of many of the country's leading families. Popayán has produced many authors, composers, painters, and other artists. It also has produced more presidents than has any other Colombian city—17 at last count (2007). Unfortunately, in 1983, a devastating earthquake struck the city and destroyed many of its oldest and finest structures.

Cali was founded in 1536, making it one of the oldest inland European cities in Latin America. Throughout most of its history, Cali was a small, quiet, remote mountain town. All this changed during the latter part of the nineteenth century, when sugar and coffee growing began to bring prosperity to the Cauca Valley. Today, Cali is Colombia's third-largest city, with a population of slightly more than 2 million inhabitants. It is also one of the country's chief economic centers. Industrial products include pharmaceuticals, foods (particularly sugar) and beverages, computer software, and machinery. As you would expect for a city of its size, Cali also specializes in providing many services. Because African slaves were introduced to work the sugar plantations, the city has one of the highest black populations in all of mainland Spanish-settled Latin America—about 30 percent.

From the late 1960s through the 1990s, Cali was a major center of the illegal trade in narcotics, particularly cocaine. The lure of drug money—amounting to billions of dollars—established a powerful elite class. It also fatally corrupted the city's social and political systems, resulting in what Colombian president Álvaro Uribe described as "social fracture." During the 1980s, it is estimated that the Cali Cartel supplied as much as 80 percent of the cocaine that reached the United States and Canada. Since the late 1990s, the power and influence of the cartel have supposedly been sharply reduced. Nonetheless, if up to 90 percent of the illegal cocaine reaching the United States comes from Colombia, some group is responsible, and a good bet is that the trade originates in Cali.

THE PASTO REGION

South of Popayán is a rugged area often called the "Pasto Knot." Here, the single-range Andean backbone splits into the three distinct ranges—Western, Central, and Eastern—that extend northward toward the Caribbean. The area is isolated from the remainder of Colombia; in fact, in many respects, it has closer ties to neighboring Ecuador, with which it is linked by the Pan American Highway. Few Europeans settled in the Pasto Region, so its population is predominantly Amerindian.

Pasto, with a population approaching 500,000 people, is the largest city in the region. It is located at the base of the 14,000-foot (4,267-meter) volcanic Mount Galeras, nestled away in the Atriz valley at an elevation of about 8,300 feet (2,530 meters). (In this context, it is important to remember that "mile-high" Denver, Colorado, at 5,280 feet (1,609 meters) is the highest city of any size in the United States.) The Pasto region

The Pasto region of Colombia is located in the southwestern part of the country, near the border with Ecuador. The region is an important producer of dairy products, and only a limited amount of farming takes places due to the rugged terrain, which is pictured here.

specializes in dairy products and manufacturing, particularly furniture. Much of its trade is with Ecuador, rather than with regions elsewhere in Colombia.

PACIFIC COASTAL LOWLAND AND ATRATO VALLEY

The region of Colombia that faces the Pacific Ocean is a narrow, coastal lowland isolated from the rest of the country. To the east are the towering Andes, which create a huge barrier.

Over a north-south distance of approximately 300 miles (483 kilometers), only two roads descend from the highlands to the coast. The northern half of the lowland is drained northward into the Gulf of Urabá and the Caribbean Sea by the Atrato River. The region holds one rather unenviable distinction—it has one of Earth's most soggy and sweltering climates. Temperatures average approximately 80°F (26.7°C) year round, with little seasonal or day-to-day variation, and is it ever wet! *Officially*, Quibdó, located on the Atrato River southwest of Medellín, is the rainiest spot on the mainland of the Americas. But *unofficially*, Lloro, a small community located a short distance from Quibdó, holds the world record for annual precipitation. Its current average rainfall is 524 inches (13,310 millimeters)!

Much of the region is covered by rainforest or swamp. There is little farmland, and few minerals have drawn people into the coastal lowland. As was noted, east-west surface routes are all but nonexistent, and in a north-south direction, no roads exist at all. The Atrato River does provide a water route from its valley settlements to the Caribbean lowlands and coast, however. All things considered, it is little wonder that even today fewer than 4 percent of all Colombians inhabit the region. Most residents are of African origin or of mixed black and Amerindian ancestry. Few people of European descent chose to make this region their home.

The only city of any size is the port of Buenaventura, which has a population of about 325,000. It has the advantage of being the only lowland city with reliable surface transportation linkages to the interior. Both a railroad and paved highway provide access to the interior at Cali and beyond. Because of these facilities, Buenaventura is now Colombia's major seaport on the Pacific Ocean and also its primary port for coffee exports. Unfortunately, during recent years, the city has been plagued by violence, giving Buenaventura the dubious distinction of now being Colombia's "murder capital." During the past several years, the city's murder rate has soared to nearly

25 times that of even the worst U.S. communities. Much of the problem stems from the city's growing role as a major center for drug trafficking.

THE ORIENTE

The final region we will visit in our quick tour of Colombia is larger than all seven others combined—the Eastern Tropical Lowlands, Eastern Plains, or *Oriente*. This huge area, about the size of Texas or any of Canada's Prairie Provinces, is a world unto itself. Nowhere does an all-season road cross the entire region. Those few roads that do exist are passable only during the dry season, and the southern half of the Oriente, an area about the size of New Mexico, has no roads whatsoever. Low population, isolation, and limited economic activity are three key facts to keep in mind about this region. In addition, the population is composed primarily of Amerindians representing many languages and tribal groups. The few Europeans living in the Oriente are involved mainly in political administration, economic development, or as clergy.

Geographers have divided the Oriente into two subregions. The northern roughly two-thirds of the area lies within the upper drainage of the Orinoco River. Its seasonal wet-and-dry climate supports a savanna ecosystem called the Llanos (ya-nos). Tall grasses, shrubs, and scattered trees are ideal for livestock grazing. Ranching has long been the primary economic activity of the grasslands. Herds are watched over by *llaneros*, nearly all of whom are Amerindian or mestizo. These skilled horsemen have contributed to the creation of legends, as did the cowboys of the American West and the *gauchos* of the Pampa region of Argentina.

The southern third of the Oriente lies within the upper drainage of the Amazon River. Here, a humid tropical climate contributes to a *selva* (tropical rainforest) ecosystem. All long-distance transportation in the area is either by water or air because land routes do not exist. Traditionally, the only "industry" has been the gathering of tropical products, including latex (rubber). The only community of any size is Leticia. This city of about 25,000 residents is located at the point where the borders of Peru, Brazil, and Colombia meet. It also has the advantage of sitting on the upper Amazon River, allowing it to be a local trade center, although only air and river boat linkages exist to the outside world. Despite being located about 2,000 miles (3,218 kilometers) upstream from the mouth of the mighty Amazon, ocean-going vessels reach Leticia and beyond (to Iquitos, Peru).

8

Colombia Looks Ahead

C olombia is a baffling country, perhaps more so than any other in Latin America. It has tremendous potential. Nature, people, and culture provide a solid foundation on which a strong, stable, prosperous future can be built. Socially, politically, and economically, however, the country has been and continues to fall far short of its potential. Colombians look ahead with hope and optimism but toward a future that remains uncertain.

If, indeed, the past provides clues to the future, the outlook for Colombia is not good. Colombians can look back upon nearly a half-millennium of almost constant conflict. Some drawbacks, such as natural hazards and physical features that tend to divide the country, are beyond human control. Much greater obstacles stand in the way of the country ever achieving stability and experiencing progress, however. Existing social, economic, and political systems are frail. Crime and violence continue to plague the population. Many if not most of the country's current problems, of course, are directly related to two primary factors. The first is the huge gap that exists between the wealthy power elite and the poor and powerless. The second, and most challenging, is the ongoing international drug trade and the tremendous power of those who control it. These two obstacles exert a strongly negative impact on existing social, economic, and political systems.

In the rest of this chapter, we will review the way(s) in which each topic discussed in previous chapters may influence Colombia's future, beginning with the natural environment. Little can be done to avoid many of the country's devastating environmental hazards. The Andes, after all, lie squarely on the Pacific Rim of Fire, which is the world's largest zone of geologic instability. Violent volcanic eruptions and devastating earthquakes have happened on many occasions in the past. Certainly, they shall continue to wreak havoc. As the population expands, an increasing number of people will be vulnerable to their wrath. Periodic droughts and occasional severe floods will also continue. The effect of a warming earth remains a giant question mark in regard to the wet tropical and wet-and-dry tropical climates.

Colombia's natural environment also offers many positive conditions on which the country can build. Its has good harbors on both the Atlantic and Pacific coasts, and the country's location places it closer to the United States and the Panama Canal than any other South American country. Because of its mountainous terrain and vertical climate zones, the country experiences many microclimates. This presents a huge advantage in that a wide variety of crops from tropical to upper-middle latitudes can be grown. Mountain valleys and coastal plains offer fertile volcanic ash–derived, or alluvial, soils. There are ample natural grasslands for grazing livestock. Caribbean beaches (particularly near Santa Marta) offer great tourist potential. So do spectacular mountain scenery and the fascinating tropical rainforests and savannas—with windows

In the coming years, the Colombian government will have to curtail the production of cocaine if it hopes to achieve political stability. Here, Colombian police spray herbicides on coca plants in the suburbs of Medellín, the country's second-largest city.

on two of the world's mightiest rivers, the Orinoco and Amazon. The country has abundant mineral wealth, including the continent's richest coal deposits.

Historically, there is little to set Colombia apart from most other Latin American countries. A native population was conquered by European (in this case, Spanish) invaders with the usual results: declining native populations; eventual racial mixing, contributing to a dominant (in Colombia) mestizo population; conversion to Roman Catholicism and other European cultural practices; and the imposition of a feudal system that continues to affect society, government, and economy. In some respects, Colombians have been more successful than many other Latinos in moving beyond this heritage. For example, *machismo* never took deep root in Colombia, and rather than avoiding manual labor, many residents of European heritage welcome hard work.

Population and settlement pose few major obstacles to future stability and development. The rate of population increase (1.18 percent) is now comparable to the world average and far below that of most less-developed countries. With the third-largest population in Latin America and a literacy rate of about 92 percent, the country has ample human resources with which to develop economically.

With regard to settlement, it is true that huge areas—particularly the Pacific coastal lowland and Oriente—remain isolated from the rest of the country. Isolation, however, is not really a physical condition. Rather, it is the result of a lack of economic incentives to draw settlers into an area. This, in turn, contributes to a lack of infrastructure and other amenities, which further contribute to isolation. Assuming Colombia can eventually overcome its current conflicts, the country's economy will surely grow. When this occurs, capital resources to invest in the further development of the country's regional potentials will become available.

In many respects, a stable and effective government is the key to any country's stability. This becomes evident when one looks over the list of countries at the top and bottom of various country rankings. (For example, see the Human Development Index, or Transparency International Corruption Perceptions Index.) Colombia, perhaps more so than most other Latin American countries, has a tradition of democratic government. Unfortunately, the parties engaged in the country's two-party

Colombia's future lies in the hands of its youth: The median age of its citizens is only 27.6, and 27 percent of the population is 14 years old or younger. Here, Colombian children take part in a demonstration supporting peace in Bogotá.

political system (liberals and conservatives) have fought bitterly against one another on various occasions. Today, however, such conflict appears to be a thing of the past. All of the necessary components of good government are in place; they simply need to be allowed to function successfully.

In terms of total Gross Domestic Product, Colombia's (legal) economy is the third strongest in South America, trailing only Brazil and Argentina, and twenty-eighth in the world. Were the illegal drug trade factored into the equation, certainly the country would rank much higher. This is remarkable, considering the many problems with which the country has been beset during the past half century. If the drug issue can be resolved, and the government is free to address the needs of the Colombian people and the country's development, the economy should boom. Tourism offers a potential source of revenue. Proximity to the United States, Canada, and Mexico makes more than 450 million people just a short flight away. The country's rich history, diverse cultures, marvelous scenery, varied environments, and Caribbean beaches are among the attractions. Finally, Colombia's current strong sectionalism, which often pits one region against another, is gradually breaking down as transportation and communication links improve.

It is essential that all Colombians—regardless of region of residence, race or ethnicity, political affiliation, socioeconomic status, or other divisions—work together for the good of all. Before this can happen, however, the potentially fatal sickness inflicted by the international drug trade must be cured. If this can be accomplished—and it remains a big "if"—the other essential elements that contribute to stability should fall into place. Based on a number of developments during recent years, there are reasons for optimism. You will know that the country is progressing when headlines such as those appearing at the beginning of Chapter 1 are but a distant memory.

Facts at a Glance

Unless otherwise indicated, all data are mid-2010 estimates.

Physical Geography

Location Northern South America, bordering the Caribbean Sea, between Panama and Venezuela, and bordering the Pacific Ocean, between Ecuador and Panama

Area 440,831 square miles (1,141,747 square kilometers), slightly smaller than combined area of Texas, New Mexico, and Oklahoma; *land:* 401,044 square miles (1,038,700 square kilometers); *water:* 39,691 square miles (100,210 square kilometers)

Boundaries 3,920 miles (6,309 kilometers) of land border; Venezuela, 1,274 miles (2,050 kilometers); Peru, 1,118 miles (1,800 kilometers); Brazil, 1,022 miles (1,644 kilometers); Panama, 140 miles (225 kilometers); and Ecuador, 367 miles (590 kilometers); borders Atlantic Ocean and Caribbean Sea, 1,218 miles (1,760 kilometers) and Pacific Ocean, 900 miles (1,448 kilometers)

Climate Tropical lowlands and highlands; elevation is primary control of temperature; Pacific coastal and eastern lowlands experience humid tropical climatic conditions; portions of northern coast are seasonally wet and dry tropical

Terrain Northern Andean highlands divided into several separate ranges separated by fertile river valleys; approximately one-half of territory composed of eastern lowland plains; narrow Pacific and Atlantic lowland plains

Elevation Extremes Lowest point is the Pacific Ocean, sea level; highest point is Pico Cristóbal Colón and Pico Simón Bolívar, both of which are believed to reach approximately 18,950 feet (5,776 meters)

Land Use Arable land, 2.01%; permanent crops, 1.37%; other, 96.62% (2005)

Irrigated Land 3,475 square miles (9,000 square kilometers) (2003)

Natural Hazards Highlands subject to often devastating volcanic eruptions and earthquakes; occasional droughts

Natural Resources Coal, petroleum, natural gas, and hydropower; iron ore, nickel, gold, copper, and emeralds; tropical forests

Environmental Issues	Deforestation; soil and water quality damage from overuse of pesticides; air pollution, especially in Bogotá, from vehicle emissions

People

Population	44,205,293
Population Density	100 per square mile (39 per square kilometer)
Settlement	74% urban; 26% rural
Population Growth Rate	1.18 percent
Net Migration Rate	-0.68 migrant(s)/1,000 population
Total Fertility Rate	2.2 children given birth by average woman during her lifetime (2.1 is replacement rate)
Birthrate	17.8 births per 1,000 population
Death Rate	5.2 deaths per 1,000 population
Life Expectancy at Birth	Total Population: 74.3 years (male, 71.0 years; female, 77.8 years)
Median Age	Total: 27.6 years; male, 26.7 years; female, 28.6 years
Racial and Ethnic Groups	Mestizo, 58%; white, 20% (dominantly of Spanish ancestry); mulatto (black and white mixed ancestry), 14%; black, 4%; mixed black-Amerindian, 3%; Amerindian, 1%
Religions	Roman Catholic, 90%; Protestant, 1%; other or none 9%
Age Structure	0–14 years, 27.2%; 15–64 years, 66.8%; 65 years and older, 6%
Languages	Spanish, although small groups of Amerindians (less than one percent of the population) speak their own tongue
Literacy	(Age 15 and older can read and write) Total Population: 92.5% (male, 92.4%; female, 92.6%)
Human Development Index	Seventy-seventh among the world's 182 rated countries (2009)

Economy

Currency	Colombian peso (COP)
GDP Purchasing Power Parity	$401 billion (2009 est.)
Rate of Economic Growth	-0.1%
GDP-PPP Per Capita	$9,200 (2009 est.)

Labor Force	21.53 million (2009 est.)
Unemployment	12% (rate of underemployment is much higher)
Population below Poverty Line	46.8% (2008)
Labor Force by Occupation	Services, 63%; agriculture, 18%; industry, 19% (2009 est.)
GDP by Sector	Services, 53%; agriculture, 10%; industry, 37% (2009 est.)
Agriculture Products	Coffee, cut flowers, bananas, rice, tobacco, corn, sugarcane, cocoa beans, oilseed, vegetables; forest products; farmed shrimp; world's largest producer of undocumented coca (cocaine)
Industries	Textiles, food processing, oil, clothing and footwear, beverages, chemicals, cement; gold, coal, emeralds
Exports	$34.03 billion (2009 est.)
Export Commodities	Petroleum, coffee, coal, nickel, emeralds, apparel, bananas, cut flowers
Imports	$31.47 billion (2009 est.)
Import Commodities	Industrial equipment, transportation equipment, consumer goods, chemicals, paper products, fuels, electricity
Leading Trade Partners	Exports: U.S., 38%; Venezuela, 16%; Ecuador, 4%; Imports: United States, 29%; China, 12%, Mexico, 8%; Brazil, 5%
Transportation	Roadways: 102,065 miles (164,257 kilometers) of which about 15% are paved; Railways: 2,362 miles (3,802 kilometers); Airports: 992–116 have paved runways; Waterways: 11,185 miles (18,000 kilometers)

Government

Country Name	Conventional long form: Republic of Colombia; Conventional short form: Colombia; Local long form: Republica de Colombia; Local short form: Colombia
Capital City	Bogotá
Type of Government	Republic; executive branch dominates government structure
Head of Government	President Juan Manuel Santos (since August 7, 2010)
Independence	July 20, 1810 (from Spain)

Administrative Divisions	32 departments (departamentos, singular–departamento) and one capital district* (distrito capital); Amazonas, Antioquia, Arauca, Atlantico, Bogotá*, Bolivar, Boyacá, Caldas, Caquetá, Casanare, Cauca, Cesar, Chocó, Córdoba, Cundinamarca, Guainia, Guaviare, Huila, La Guajira, Magdalena, Meta, Nariño, Norte de Santander, Putumayo, Quindío, Risaralda, San Andres y Providencia, Santander, Sucre, Tolima, Valle del Cauca, Vaupés, Vichada
Constitution	July 5, 1991; amended many times
Branches of Government	Executive: President and Vice President, elected to office by popular vote for four-year terms (eligible for second term); Legislative: bicameral (two houses) Congress consisting of 102-member Senate and 166-member House of Representatives (members of both serve four-year terms); Judicial: four roughly coequal, supreme judicial organs; Supreme Court of Justice (highest court of criminal law), Council of State (highest court of administrative law), Constitutional Court (guards integrity and supremacy of the constitution; rules on constitutionality of laws, amendments to the constitution, and international treaties); Superior Judicial Council (administers and disciplines the civilian judiciary; resolves jurisdictional conflicts arising between other courts)

Communications

TV Stations	60
Radio Stations:	515 (454 AM, 34 FM, 27 shortwave)
Phones	(Line) 6,820,000; (cell) 41,365,000 (2008)
Internet Users	17,117,000 (2008)

* Primary Source: *CIA-The World Factbook* (2010)

B.C.

< 20,000   Evidence suggests earliest human presence.

500   Tairona civilization flourishes and establishes city of Teyuna (now Ciudad Perdida ["Lost City"], east of present-day Santa Marta).

A.D.

1000–1541   Chibcha (Muisca) culture flourishes in vicinity of present-day Bogotá until conquered by the Spanish.

Early 1500   Spanish begin exploration of Caribbean coastal mainland.

1525   Spanish establish second permanent settlement in South America at Santa Marta, the site of a fine natural harbor on Colombia's Caribbean coast.

1533   Cartagena is founded as a port city from which gold and other wealth are shipped to Spain.

1536–1538   Conquistador Gonzalo Jiménez de Quesada leads expedition into the Andes and finds substantial amounts of gold and emeralds.

1538   Quesada founds Santa Fe de Bogotá (present-day Bogotá).

1550   Quesada is appointed marshal of New Granada and councilor of Bogotá; African slaves begin to arrive in Colombia to work on plantations.

1575–1625   Tairona peoples, forced by the Spanish to convert to Catholicism, flee the coast and move into the Andean mountains.

1718   Spain combines Colombia with neighboring territories Ecuador, Venezuela, and Panama into one large colony called the Viceroyalty of New Granada.

1810   Colombia gains independence from Spain on July 20.

1819   General Simón Bolívar defeats royalist forces in the Battle of Boyaca on August 7; the Republic of Colombia (also known as Gran Colombia and consisting of Colombia, Ecuador, and Venezuela) is proclaimed on December 17, with Simón Bolivar as the first president.

1830   Ecuador and Venezuela break away from Gran Colombia, leaving Colombia and Panama as Nueva Granada.

1853   Colombia abolishes slavery.

1899–1902	Civil war called the "War of a Thousand Days" takes place between liberals and conservatives, resulting in the loss of an estimated 120,000 lives.
1903	With U.S. backing, Panama secedes from Colombia, allowing the United States to gain control over the Isthmus of Panama, now the Panama Canal Zone.
1922	The United States pays Colombia $25 million for the loss of Panama.
1939–1945	Colombia helps the United States keep the Panama Canal open during World War II.
1948–1957	Civil war results in death of estimated 250,000 to 300,00 Colombians.
1965	Leftist National Liberation Army (ELN) and Maoist People's Liberation Army (EPL) are founded.
1966	Revolutionary Armed Forces of Colombia (FARC) is established.
1970–1971	Left-wing National People's Alliance and M-19 guerrilla groups are formed.
1970s	Influence of drug trade, drug cartels, and related atrocities rise.
1978	Government begins intensive fight against drug traffickers and cartels.
1985	Nevado del Ruiz volcano erupts, killing an estimated 23,000 people in four Andean towns.
1989	United States begins to supply military equipment to the Colombian government to help rid Colombia of drug dealers.
1999	Cities of Armenia and Pereira are devastated by powerful earthquake that kills approximately 1,000 people.
2002	After three years of intensive negotiations, talks fail between government representatives and FARC rebels.
2002	Alavaro Uribe becomes President and vows to take a strong stand against terrorists.
2006	Uribe elected to second term as President.
2010	Uribe barred from running for third term of office; Juan Manuel Santos elected President. Colombia continues to struggle in from poverty, corruption, crime, civil strife, and the influence of drug cartels, although in many respects conditions are improving.

Bibliography

Clawson, David L. *Latin America and the Caribbean: Lands and Peoples.* Dubuque, Iowa: McGraw-Hill, 2006.

Collier, Simon, Thomas E. Skidmore, and Harold Blakemore, eds. *The Cambridge Encyclopedia of Latin America and the Caribbean.* Cambridge, U.K.: Cambridge University Press, 1992.

Gritzner, Charles F. "Third World Peoples and Problems: A Cycle of Frustration," in Gail L. Hobbs, ed., *The Essence of PLACE: Geography in the K-12 Curriculum.* Los Angeles: California Geography Alliance, University of California at Los Angeles, 1987; pp. 301–313.

Gunther, John. *Inside Latin America.* New York: Harper & Row, 1966.

James, Preston E. *Latin America,* 4th ed. New York: The Odyssey Press, 1969.

Morris, Arthur. *South America.* London: Hodder and Stoughton, 1979.

Web sites (accessed July 2007)

The World Factbook—Central Intelligence Agency
https://www.cia.gov/library/publications/the-world-factbook/geos/co.html

"Frequently Asked Questions." Embassy of Colombia, Washington, D.C.
http://www.colombiaemb.org/opencms/opencms/faq/english.html

Country Reports
http://www.countryreports.org/

Countries and Their Cultures
http://www.everyculture.com/index.html

About.com
http://geography.about.com/sitesearch.htm

A Country Study: Colombia
http://lcweb2.loc.gov/frd/cs/cotoc.html

Country Profile: Colombia
http://lcweb2.loc.gov/frd/cs/profiles/Colombia.pdf

Transparency International: the Global Coalition Against Corruption
http://www.transparency.org/

The World Bank
http://web.worldbank.org

Gritzner, Charles F. *Latin America*. Philadelphia: Chelsea House, 2006.

Hylton, Forrest. *Evil Hour in Colombia*. New York: Verso, 2006.

Kohn, Michael, and Robert Landon. *Colombia*. Lonely Planet Publications, 2006.

Molano, Enrique Santos. *Colombia 360: Cities and Towns*. Bogotá, Colombia: Villegas Editores, 2007

Web sites

The World Factbook—Central Intelligence Agency
https://www.cia.gov/library/publications/the-world-factbook/geos/co.html

The History of the Republic of Colombia
http://www.hartford-hwp.com/archives/42/index-d.html

A Country Study: Colombia
http://lcweb2.loc.gov/frd/cs/cotoc.html

Picture Credits

Index

118

About the Author

CHARLES F. GRITZNER is Distinguished Professor Emeritus of Geography at South Dakota State University in Brookings. In 2010, he retired after a 50-year career of college teaching. He enjoys travel, writing, and sharing his love for and knowledge of geography with readers. Gritzner has contributed to Chelsea House's MODERN WORLD NATIONS, MAJOR WORLD CULTURES, EXTREME ENVIRONMENTS, and GLOBAL CONNECTIONS series. He has served as both President and Executive Director of the National Council for Geographic Education (NCGE) and has received the Council's highest honor, the George J. Miller Award for Distinguished Service to Geographic Education, as well as numerous other national teaching, service, and research recognitions from the NCGE, the Association of American Geographers, and other organizations. Gritzner lives in South Dakota with his wife, Yvonne, and their "family" of two Italian Greyhounds.